simply better food for your
baby and children

About the author

Peter Vaughan is a graduate of the Academy of Culinary Arts and has worked in many top-class hotels and restaurants around the world. He has received many awards, including the prestigious Annual Award of Excellence.

He owns and runs The Healthy Life, a natural food shop and café, and The Bistro, a restaurant, in Devizes, Wiltshire. His policy is to use and stock products that are traded fairly and kept as close as possible to their natural state. In this way he aims to provide the healthiest diet alternatives to adults and to give children a really good start in life.

As well as running a business, he also finds time to do cookery demonstrations all round the UK and has appeared many times on television. One of his appearances was with Jenni Trent-Hughes, who has written the forward for this book. Together, they were the 'Dinner Doctors' in the Channel 5 series of the same name, where their mission was to help families with food problems, mainly connected with children's eating habits, and offer practical solutions.

Through the Academy of Culinary Arts Adopt-a-School scheme and the Wiltshire Food Challenge, Peter has worked in a number of schools, awakening children to every aspect of food and nutrition, thereby encouraging them to eat a naturally balanced diet. As a promotional chef with a well-known baby food manufacturer, he is conversant with the nutritional needs of babies and toddlers.

He is also the author of *Naturally Balanced Cooking*, published by W. Foulsham & Co. (ISBN 0-572-02826-1).

simply better food for your
baby and children

peter vaughan

foulsham
LONDON • NEW YORK • TORONTO • SYDNEY

foulsham

The Publishing House, Bennetts Close, Cippenham,
Slough, Berkshire, SL1 5AP, England

ISBN 0-572-03003-7

Photographs © 2005 W. Foulsham & Co. Ltd

Photographs by Melanie Harding

Cover photograph by Melanie Harding

A CIP record for this book is available from the British Library.

Printed in Great Britain by St Edmundsbury Press, Bury St Edmunds, Suffolk

Contents

Foreword

Over the past few years I have travelled all over the UK, working with parents and children, and trying to help in some small way to make their lives as stress-free as possible. The work has involved solving problems; providing ideas for ways by which families can improve their quality of life; and helping to show them that things can quite often be better.

Many of the issues I have to deal with are food-related. At a young age, even the most angelic of children soon learn that food can be a powerful tool in the family dynamic and they often use this knowledge to its full advantage. We all know what happens if the foundation of a child's relationship with food isn't built on solid ground from the beginning – the newspapers are full of stories of how obese we are all becoming, how unfit our children are and how the incidence of childhood medical complaints is rising. Finding information on the solution to these problems is less easy, however. But if you are looking for some way to ensure that your child doesn't become an adult riddled with health and diet issues, one thing you can do is adapt the principles Peter lays out in this book.

Simply Better Food for Your Baby and Children is designed to start you and your children on the road to a lifetime of healthy eating. Recipes and advice are all put forward in the easy-to-understand, comprehensive style that is synonymous with Peter's approach. He has seemingly limitless knowledge and boundless enthusiasm for everything to do with food. He provides information on all the relevant aspects of the subject, from tips on freezing and information on the dreaded E-numbers, to how to get the best value for your money. The recipes are straightforward and clearly laid out, and even if you're a novice in the kitchen you will be able to prepare food for your child that is nutritious, healthy and tasty. (Be sure to make the Baby Pork Burgers with Apple – I now serve them at dinner parties!) There is even a fabulous chapter on 'sanctuary time', with recipes specially designed for parents and tips on how to chill out. Not that you'll need those, if you follow Peter's advice in the rest of the book.

If you enjoyed Peter's last book, *Naturally Balanced Cooking,* then you will welcome this sequel with open arms. *Simply Better Food for Your Baby and Children* will make your life easier and your childrens' lives better. In short, it explains how to fulfil that most important, all-absorbing parental aim: to provide the best start we can for our children.

Enjoy!

Jenni Trent Hughes

Introduction

Every baby is a unique and special individual; and every parent wants the best for their baby. But with all the conflicting and apparently ever-changing advice that abounds in the media, new parents can become very confused when they start to think about what kind of diet is the best for their baby.

I used to think that cooking for babies and children was fiddly and possibly rather boring. It's not! It's straightforward, logical and can be a real joy. Children love simple food, simply prepared and served. But they also love experimenting with new flavours and textures as they grow. By introducing your child to good food, you can set him on the right road to a healthy balanced diet for life – and that's one of the most precious gifts you can give him. You may even find that thinking about your baby's diet helps you to improve your own!

It also stands to reason that if a baby is happy, the parents will be happy too, and that is wonderful for bringing balance to the whole family's meals. Children will learn that mealtimes are a shared experience and a pleasure – a brilliant gift that will set them up for a lifetime of enjoying good food.

This book presents you with a complete range of recipes, starting with first-food purées for tiny babies and moving through an ever-widening selection of interesting ingredients that introduce more exciting colours, textures and tastes as your child grows. It offers a natural progression towards recipes that will suit the whole family – including some of my favourites – making mealtimes a great time to share.

I hope you find this book useful and inspiring. Please don't worry if your baby throws food and drink all over the pages as you are trying to read them – that's his way of paying you a compliment! Be patient with him right from the start. Patience is a virtue and the more you show now, the more it will pay off later in his childhood.

By the way, you will notice that I refer to 'him' throughout the book; this is not intended to imply that girl babies are any less important. Whether your baby is a boy or a girl, I have written this book for both of you.

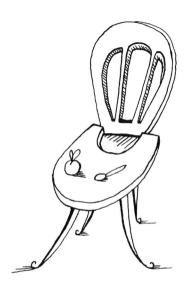

Healthy eating in a modern world

In the past, a family's food was all prepared from basic, fresh, locally grown ingredients. Not any more: many of us live life at a very fast pace nowadays, juggling any number of balls in the air all at the same time. The availability of convenience and ready-prepared foods seems to offer a welcome relief to anyone in this position. However, healthcare professionals are split in their opinions as to whether you should offer convenience and processed baby food to your child or whether you should give them freshly cooked food for every meal. The reality is that your own lifestyle will, to some extent, dictate what is suitable for you.

Balance is the key

Just like adults, babies and children need a variety of food types in their diet. As they grow, the balance of these groups will change but they will always need some of the following every day: protein for growth; carbohydrates and some fats for energy; vitamins and minerals for general good health; and plenty of liquids. These should be included in your family's meals whether they are home-made from fresh ingredients or ready-prepared convenience foods.

If you feed your children a combination of fresh and processed foods, this will help them to develop discerning palates as they grow up, and educate them to know how to find that balance that I mentioned above. Certainly, as they get older, the pace of life and speed of technological advance are not likely to slow down, and convenience foods are not going to go away. It is therefore important that they learn that there is a place for all kinds of food in their diet, and how to be selective in the balance they establish.

Convenience meals included in a wholesome diet of home-cooked food will help provide you with flexibility, speed and convenience, as well as reducing your stress levels. That can only be good for your enjoyment of food – and your baby's.

Go for organic

That said, I would always opt for organic produce whenever possible. This is because the assumptions we make – that fresh food is unadulterated – turn out sometimes not to be the case. 'Fresh' foodstuffs are frequently treated, to make them grow faster, to prevent pest damage, to make them last longer while they are transported, and for a whole host of other reasons. Often, it is only as the result of a food scare that we discover information – not necessarily pleasant – about the production of our food.

We all want the best for our family, particularly for our babies. I would always recommend using the best-quality foods you can find when preparing food for your family. That means finding foods that are as fresh as possible, which may present a problem if you can't be sure exactly where your food comes from or what it contains. However, if you went into it in too much detail, it could become a very unhealthy obsession! What you can reasonably do is aim to prepare as much food as you can from fresh ingredients that are as near to their natural state as possible. A good starting point for this is buying locally produced organic foods. Of course, that's not always possible and will also be more expensive and therefore not suitable for some families. But it is worth trying to include as much fresh produce of every kind – meat, poultry, fish, fruit and vegetables – as you can in your baby's diet.

Whole foods and unprocessed products

Processing removes many of the nutrients contained in foods so I would recommend that you use fresh, unprocessed foods wherever possible for your family. Check labels for words like 'unrefined', 'natural' and 'raw' – as in unrefined oils, natural vanilla essence and raw cane sugar.

Whole wheat and grain products, such as rice, pasta and bread, include all the essential nutrients, with nothing stripped away during the processing. Brown rice, for example, will give your child much more nourishment than white rice, which has been polished, a process that removes many nutrients. There is a well-known story of how prisoners of war in one Japanese camp appeared to be in better health than the Japanese officers in charge of them. It turned out that they were being fed on the rice husks that had been rubbed off so that the officers could eat lovely white polished rice. Little did anyone know that all the nutrients were in the husks!

Do be aware, however, that whole grains and high-fibre foods are not suitable for small babies. You will find lists of which foods are suitable for you to offer to your growing baby at the beginning of each chapter in this book.

Buying processed food

As I have said, in a perfect world, every child would eat only fresh, wholesome, home-made dishes. Some parents believe that if they prevent their small children from eating anything processed, they will never be fussy about what foods they eat, never throw a tantrum at the dinner table and not crave sugary snacks. The reality, of course, is far less predictable – and your five-year-old is unlikely to start to eat Brussels sprouts just because you've said they are good for him!

There will, I'm sure, be times when you will want to use processed foods and let your child enjoy some sweets or garishly coloured cakes at a party. That's fine! The key is simply to keep the overall balance in mind and maintain a relaxed attitude to feeding your child. Just remember that in the context of a sound, balanced diet, the odd sweet treat won't upset this – it will just add to the variety.

Food should be fun, both to prepare and to eat. Give yourself plenty of time for both – that's where convenience foods may be very helpful. Try to encourage variety and experimentation, focusing on wholesome ingredients and making mealtimes enjoyable. And, whatever you do, don't allow feeding your baby or toddler to become a battleground.

When you do buy processed foods, make sure you read the labels to find those that include the most natural ingredients and avoid additives and preservatives. Nowadays, most baby foods do not, in fact, include such unnecessary ingredients. However, as your child gets older and eats a broader range of foods, you may find additives are 'hiding' in what looks like an acceptable food or drink. For example, it is now well known that the synthetic colourings tartrazine (E102), sunset yellow (E110) and quinoline yellow (FCF E104) may have a detrimental effect on some children. The Hyperactive Children's Support group specifically recommends you avoid them, and they have also been shown to cause migraine headaches, asthmatic reactions and other allergic reactions in some people.

Step by step to real food

Your baby's diet will start with milk: one simple, unvaried food for several months. That's the easy bit. But he will then need to learn to accept and enjoy new flavours and textures. If you gradually and sensitively introduce a range of fresh and wholesome foods, your baby will develop a taste for good food that will stay with him for good. Those eating habits will not only mean that he is likely to be healthier and stronger as a child, but can also help to improve sleep patterns and good behaviour too.

By the time he is two to three years old, he will – broadly speaking – be eating a similar diet to the whole family, one that includes a wide range of tastes, textures and colours. Your job is to help him make that transition, and, as I've said, the route should be slow and smooth. To progress from a bland liquid, you'll first offer him a bland, slightly thicker purée. Once he is used to that, you can gradually introduce different flavours and thicker, more varied textures, in a simple, step-by-step process.

In this chapter we'll look at the basic stages of that process. Obviously, all babies progress at their own pace, so I've included hints on how to recognise when your baby is ready to move on. You'll find more detail on the practicalities of weaning in the next chapter, and more information on when to introduce different foods in the individual chapters.

Milk – the first meal

To a newborn baby, his mother is the first source of nourishment, the key to life. Obviously breastfeeding is the most natural option as the milk is specifically designed to give your baby everything he needs in terms of perfect nutrition. It also provides him with immunity to some conditions. In return, the mother will also receive some health benefits: breastfeeding for longer periods has been shown to reduce the risks of breast cancer. Breastfeeding also bonds mother and baby together – emotionally and physically – plus it is very convenient to have the food on tap wherever you are, with no need for rigorous sterilisation procedures!

Your midwife and health visitor will give you advice and guidance on how to breastfeed your baby – there are some techniques that will make the learning process much quicker and easier for you and the baby! – and there are plenty of books available on the subject. In the UK, you can also get practical support from the National Childbirth Trust and you can find out about their services via their website, which you can find at www.nctpregnancyandbabycare.com

That is not to say that breastfeeding is always straightforward. Some mothers find it difficult, and feeding duties can't be shared with a husband or partner. For these and other reasons some mothers decide that they prefer to feed their baby formula milk. If this is the option you choose, your midwife or health visitor will be able to give you the best advice and guidance. For example, you may find that you need to give your baby little sips of water in addition to the milk, as formula milk may not quench your baby's thirst as much as breast milk does.

Whatever you choose, the crucial thing about this vital first stage of feeding is that both you and your baby are happy with what you are doing. Feeding times should be pleasant and relaxed so both you and your baby are contented and enjoy them to the full. Even the tiniest baby can be astonishingly intuitive and will quickly pick up any feelings of anxiety at feeding times. This will make them tense and discontented so that they will not feed properly. Then, of course, they will become fractious because they will quickly become hungry again, thus repeating the cycle. They may even begin to associate feeding times with tension and anxiety.

Remember that feeding your baby, whether by breast or bottle, is only one aspect of motherhood. Stay relaxed, ask for help if you need it, and you should soon settle into a comfortable and enjoyable routine.

Ready for solid food

After the first few months of life, when milk provides the baby with all its nutritional needs, he will start to show signs that he is ready to be moved on to solid food. This is normally referred to as weaning – which always sounds rather odd to me, so call it whatever you want! It is important not to try to give your baby solid food too early because it takes around four months for the lining of the baby's gut to develop and for the kidneys to mature enough to cope with the waste products from solid food. In fact, many experts believe that one of the reasons for the rapid increase in allergies and food intolerances over the last 15 years is because babies have been weaned before their digestive systems are ready to cope.

Don't be hasty or pressured into starting your baby on solid foods too early: each one is unique. Watch your baby and he will tell you when it is time to start introducing solid food. If in doubt, ask your health visitor. As a general rule, the following apply.

- The baby will be between four and six months old.
- They will have reached a weight of about 5.4–6.3 kg (12–14 lb).
- They may start to appear to be still hungry after a milk feed and will not be pacified with more milk.
- They may wake up earlier and earlier each morning.
- Having started to sleep through the night, they may start waking again for a feed during the night.
- They may be irritable a good hour or so before a feed is due.
- They start to put their fingers, toes or toys into their mouth to chew.

Trying solids

Weaning your baby from liquids to solid foods is an exciting time so it is important to remember to be led by your baby. Do not try to rush him to the next stage before he is ready.

You should continue to feed your baby his usual breast or formula milk until he is at least six months; this will still be his main source of nourishment. In addition, you can start to offer a little very thin, runny purée made with baby rice, once a day. Simply mix the baby rice – an excellent first food – with a little formula or expressed breast milk, or with cooled boiled water. Remember that your baby is only used to the taste of milk, so start with a very bland flavour.

Also remember that his only experience of feeding is milk, and so will try to suck the new food off the spoon, like a liquid. For this reason, you must not make it too thick. Don't worry that the food is just a soft, dribbly mush – that's exactly how your baby will like it!

Soft purées

As your baby becomes used to the baby rice, you can make the mixture a little thicker and once your baby has got used to that, it is time to move on to feeding him a soft purée of other foods. If you introduce each new stage at a slow and relaxed pace, it will go much more smoothly. Offer only one new flavour at a time, making sure that each one is still fairly bland – potato and avocado are good. That way, he can get used to the taste of each single ingredient, one at a time. There is an interesting choice of both tastes and colours for him to try: carrot, butternut squash, parsnip and broccoli all work well. If there is something he clearly doesn't like, take it off the menu for a couple of months, then try introducing it again.

Start to decrease the amount of milk you add to the mixture so that you are feeding him a soft purée. Do make sure, though, that the food is still thoroughly liquidised, with no lumps.

Once the baby has become used to the flavour of each vegetable on its own, you could then start to combine them. At this stage your baby will be starting to recognise the different tastes and learning to differentiate between sweet, sour, salty and bitter. Note that you should not add any kind of seasoning or flavouring – the flavours naturally contained in the vegetables are quite sufficient and added salt will overload immature kidneys.

Coping with lumps

At somewhere around eight months, you can begin to process your purées slightly less finely, leaving a few soft lumps in the mixture. You will find that your baby is beginning to chew foods rather than just sucking in and swallowing them, so now you can gradually be more adventurous. At this age, your baby will also begin to enjoy holding small pieces of food and feeding himself. You can offer rusks and other finger foods that will 'melt' in the mouth, even small pieces of mild cheese, for example.

As always, be guided by your baby.

Foods to avoid

Not every kind of food is suitable for young babies. Their digestive systems are too immature to cope with some foods, so you will find that the recipes in the first chapter in this book are based almost exclusively around cooked fruit and vegetables. You may wish to experiment with other ingredients, but the list below shows specific foods that should be avoided when first introducing solid food. You will find more information about when to introduce these foods in the later chapters of this book. The following should not be given to your baby yet.

- Eggs
- Citrus fruits
- Cows' milk and other dairy products
- Fruit juices and squashes
- High-fibre foods such as brown rice and whole-grain cereals
- Honey
- Hot spices
- Meat and poultry
- Nuts
- Shellfish
- Wheat products

As adults, we tend to add lots of extra flavourings to our food, in order to give it more taste or to make it more palatable. However, this should be avoided when you make baby food. Two seemingly innocuous substances in particular should be avoided.

Salt: This is completely unnecessary in a baby's food. It puts a strain on young kidneys and can encourage your child to develop a taste for salt rather than the natural flavour of the food. Some processed foods, such as stock cubes, are very high in salt so are best not used in cooking for babies and young children.

Sugar: This offers only extra calories without any nutritional value. Too much sugar will damage a baby's developing teeth and it should be kept to an absolute minimum so that the baby does not develop a preference for over-sweet foods. There are plenty of naturally sweet foods that a baby will enjoy, then, as they grow older, you can introduce sweet foods as part of a naturally balanced diet.

It is best to avoid giving both salt and sugar to your child at all – or certainly only include them in small quantities when they are older. In this way, they will not get used to those tastes and it will be much easier for you to maintain a healthy balanced diet for them as they grow.

Drinks

As you progress to mixed feeding, your baby will gradually demand fewer milk feeds but milk will still be an important part of his diet. To begin with, this will be breast or formula milk, which the Department of Health recommends should be given to babies throughout their first year. By six months, you can start to substitute follow-on milk formula, which contains iron and vitamins in a form that is easy to digest. Cows' milk should not be given as a main drink before one year as it does not contain these in sufficient quantities. After one year, you can switch to cow's milk. This should be full-fat, not skimmed or semi-skimmed, and your baby should have a minimum of 350 ml/⅔ pt/1⅓ cups a day.

Apart from the milk that makes up his meals, your baby will probably want other drinks too, particularly if the weather is hot. Babies under six months can be given cooled, boiled tap water or bottled water. Do not boil the water repeatedly, as this will concentrate the mineral salts in it.

When your baby is six months old, you can start offering fruit juices, such as apple or orange. These should be unsweetened and diluted one part juice to three parts water. Offer them with, rather than between, meals, as fruit juice contains acids that may damage the teeth. There are also fruit drinks that are manufactured specially for babies, but many of these contain surprising amounts of sugar - in fact anything that is labelled 'drink' rather than 'juice' will almost certainly be sweetened. Check the labels and avoid anything that contains sugar, sucrose, lactose, glucose, dextrose, maltose or honey.

The following drinks should never be given to babies under one year old.

- Bottled water that is labelled 'natural mineral water': this contains a high level of mineral salts.
- Fizzy drinks: these are very acidic, often very sweet and tend to contain artificial flavourings, colourings and preservatives.
- Coffee and tea: both are stimulants that speed up the heart rate and interfere with nutrient absorption of nutrients.

The practicalities of weaning

Weaning is no different from breast- or bottle-feeding in that it works best in a relaxed and calm environment. If you keep everything as comfortable and familiar as possible and progress gradually, then the whole process will be natural and stress-free.

The first feeds

When you introduce solid food for the first time, do so at a feed when your baby is awake and fairly hungry. Mid-morning or lunchtime feeds are therefore best. This also enables you to monitor any adverse reactions to foods, in the unlikely event there are any foods your baby cannot tolerate (see page 23).

Make sure your hands are thoroughly clean. Make up about 15 ml/1 tbsp of baby rice according to the packet directions. This is more than you will need – you should only expect the baby to eat about 5 ml/1 tsp to start with, as much of it will be dribbled out rather than swallowed. The food should be just lukewarm (see page 21). Test it on your own tongue, using a separate spoon, to make absolutely sure it is not too hot.

Hold the baby in your arms, exactly as you would to feed him from the breast or bottle, so he feels safe and secure. Cover him with a bib and have a warm, damp flannel handy to wipe up any mess.

Give the baby a small amount of breast or formula milk to take the edge off his hunger. You can then offer him a little baby rice.

As babies can only suck food, there are two ways to do this. You can either dip a clean little finger into the food and then tempt the baby to suck on it, or put a tiny bit of food on the tip of a baby spoon and hold it to your baby's lips and let him suck it off. Don't bring the spoon up to his mouth from the side and surprise him – bring the food gradually towards his mouth from the front, so that he can see it as it comes towards his mouth. Don't put the spoon into his mouth, just rest it on his lip so he can suck off the food.

Once you have given the rice, finish with the rest of the milk feed.

Go at your baby's pace

If your baby turns away his head, he has probably had enough. Never force him to take more food than he wants. If your baby clearly does not want the rice and becomes upset, just stop. Give the normal breast- or bottle-feed, then try again after a few days.

Increasing quantities

Gradually build up the amount you give the baby at this feed to about 10–15 ml/2–3 tsp of food. When he is happy with that, you can move on to giving two solid feeds a day. You can then gradually increase the number of solid feeds and the quantity as your baby grows.

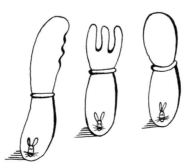

Making purées

This is easy: all you have to do is start off thin, then make them thicker and lumpier as the baby gets older and can cope – it doesn't exactly demand huge culinary skills at the beginning! The recipes on pages 33–44 give you full instructions but for now, here is how it goes…

To make a basic purée, cook the food until it is thoroughly soft, then purée it with a hand-held blender or in a liquidiser or food processor. If you don't have any of these labour-saving gadgets, simply use the back of a wooden spoon to rub it through a fairly fine-meshed sieve (strainer).

You can adjust the thickness with a little liquid – either breast or formula milk, or cooled, boiled water. Add a little at a time until you have the thickness you want. As your baby grows and his needs change, gradually reduce the amount of liquid you add to the mixture. When he is about six months old and can cope with more texture, try liquidising for a shorter time and leave some lumps in the food, although you should still make sure they are soft enough to break up in his mouth.

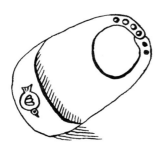

Cooking in quantity

Making baby-sized meals is rather time-consuming, but there are easy ways round this. Cooking in larger quantities and then freezing into ready-to-serve feed sizes is by far the most cost-effective and time-saving way to make food for your child. However, don't make too much at one time. While it is much more sensible to cook and prepare a small pan full of carrots, for example, you should remember that the quantities you need – especially at the start – are very tiny. There is no point in cooking and preparing and freezing large quantities or you won't be able to use up the food while it is at its best.

Preparing and freezing food for your baby is simple. Cook, strain, then purée the food as you would normally. Cool it as quickly as possible by standing the pan in a bowl of cold – preferably iced – water. When it is completely cold, place in sterilised ice-cube trays. Transfer the trays to the freezer to freeze solid overnight. The next day, turn them out on to a clean plate, then transfer them to a freezer bag. Seal the bag and label it with the contents and, more importantly, the date. Fruit and vegetable purées will keep safely in the freezer for up to four months. Meat, chicken or fish purées will keep well for up to two months but purées containing milk will only keep for up to six weeks.

Most foods that you would prepare for your baby will freeze perfectly well. However, there are a few that don't: bananas, avocado, potatoes (on their own) and melons should not be frozen.

Heating baby food

Your baby is used to food at body temperature, and that's how you should serve it at the beginning. A baby's mouth is obviously very sensitive and cannot tolerate food that is too warm, let alone hot.

When you are making baby rice, use slightly cooled, boiled water to mix it up (see the packet directions), then leave it to cool to the right temperature before you feed the baby. When you start to cook and purée your own meals for the baby, by the time you have drained and processed the food, it should have cooled to about the right temperature.

Whatever you do, always test the temperature of the food before you give it to your baby. Test it on your own tongue, using a separate spoon. It should not feel either hot or cold – just body temperature.

Reheating baby food

If you have puréed cold food and need to heat it up, you can simply warm it in a small saucepan or in a microwave, then stir it well to make sure that it is evenly heated through. Alternatively, you can warm it in a heatproof bowl set in a pan of hot water.

Take care when reheating frozen food for your baby. Either transfer it to a covered container in the fridge to defrost slowly, or defrost it in a microwave or saucepan. Remember that, since the quantities are small, it will defrost quite quickly. Once

defrosted, reheat until piping hot, then leave to cool to the correct temperature.

Always test the temperature of reheated food before you offer it to your baby to make absolutely sure it has cooled to lukewarm before serving.

Never reheat any food more than once, and never re-freeze food once it has thawed.

Sitting up for meals

After a few months when the baby is used to feeding, you may find it easier to feed him in a portable car seat or baby chair on the floor.

Once he can sit up well – at about seven months – it will be time to move into a high chair with a safety harness. This is the stage at which it starts to get really messy, as the baby will be learning to feed himself. Cover the floor under the high chair with a few sheets of old newspaper. Then, when feeding time at the zoo is over, you can simply pick it up and throw the whole lot away. Mess is all part of bringing up children and part of the learning process. If you don't let them handle food and use spoons – because they get food everywhere – they will not be able to learn to master the technique and it will simply make the whole process take much longer. It will also raise everyone's stress levels and spoil all your efforts to make mealtimes relaxed and enjoyable. So, whatever you do, don't get precious about your interior decor when your baby decides to throw food at the wall. It's a phase and it will pass!

Food allergies and intolerances

Comparatively few children suffer adverse reactions to foods, so most parents will be unlikely to have to deal with any allergies or intolerances. Moreover, for those children who do have adverse reactions, the symptoms are unlikely to be severe, so while parents should be vigilant, there is no need to be unduly concerned.

However, in a very few cases, an allergy or food intolerance may cause serious difficulties, so it is important to be aware of possible symptoms just in case you encounter a problem. Those with a family history of allergies should obviously be slightly more vigilant as it is possible for some problems to be passed on from parent to child.

An allergy occurs when the body reacts adversely to a particular substance, known as an allergen. Symptoms of an allergic reaction vary widely, but the most usual are red blotches on the skin, swelling of the face, eyes, mouth and tongue, nausea, vomiting or diarrhoea. A baby will not necessarily show all these symptoms, and any reaction is likely to be mild initially, but may become more severe if the food is given to the child again. The most common causes of allergic reactions in babies and children are gluten (which is found in wheat), egg whites, cows' milk, nuts (especially peanuts), sesame seeds, shellfish and strawberries.

This is why it is important to introduce new foods to a child one at a time, and also why it is a good idea to begin feeding solids at breakfast or lunchtime rather than in the evening so that you are immediately aware of any problems that do occur.

While a baby's organs are still maturing, they will not be able to digest certain foods, so it is important that you do not introduce them too early. I have given more information about individual foods in later chapters.

Food intolerances differ slightly from allergies. They occur when the baby's digestive system does not produce the enzymes necessary to break down certain foods in the body. The enzyme may be absent at birth, or its production may have been affected by an illness.

The most common food intolerance is to lactose (the sugar found in milk), and the most likely symptom is an upset stomach.

If your child has any kind of reaction to any food, stop giving that food straight away, and seek advice from your health visitor or GP. Obviously, if your baby suffers a severe reaction of any kind, call emergency medical help immediately.

Equipment for making baby food

Don't be fooled by the advertisers into thinking you need to re-equip your entire kitchen in order to make your own baby food. You'll probably have almost everything you need in your kitchen already.

Baby essentials

Spoons

Ordinary teaspoons will not do for feeding a small baby. You will need some plastic baby spoons, which are soft and rounded with a very shallow bowl so they will not hurt delicate and tender gums. It's worth having several, as once your baby starts to feed himself, they'll be dropped on the floor regularly.

Dishes

Any little dish will do to start with but once your baby starts to feed himself, unbreakable crockery is essential – it will be dropped as regularly as the spoons! You can buy bowls with suction pads to stick them to a table – these are excellent once the baby is in a high chair and can throw things further!

Bibs

Whatever your baby's age, you will need to put a bib on him before feeding – the bigger, the better. Bibs with sleeves are really useful and give best protection. Fabric bibs are best for tiny babies as they are soft and comfortable; plastic-backed fabric bibs are more practical once they get a bit bigger. For older babies, you may prefer to use plastic 'pelican' bibs with a lip to catch spills.

Training beakers

Beakers with a lid and spout help your baby learn to use a cup. How anyone managed without them, I'm not sure! They also usually have a separate lid so that when you go out, you can always have a drink on hand.

Baby chairs

Baby chairs for small babies should support their back and neck and allow them to sit safely and well supported before they can sit unaided.

Once your baby's back neck muscles are strong enough and he can sit up well on his own, you will need a high chair. There are all types of design, so shop around to find something that suits your needs and your budget. Make sure that it is stable with a secure safety harness and that the fabric of the seat is washable! Once your child is about two years old, he will be able to use a booster seat strapped to an ordinary chair.

Steriliser

You will need to sterilise your baby's bottles and equipment. You can simply boil them in water but this is messy, time-consuming and none too safe. It is easier to buy a specially designed steriliser (see page 28).

Cooking utensils

Small saucepan
A small pan with a lid is vital for cooking small quantities of food with just a small amount of liquid.

Mouli or metal-mesh sieve (strainer)
Both of these are useful tools for making puréed foods and eliminating any indigestible fibrous husks or skins.

Liquidiser
I would recommend that you use a small hand-held electric blender. These are easy to use for small quantities and very inexpensive. If you don't have one already, ask for one as a baby-arrival gift! Of course, if you have a liquidiser or food processor, these are very effective too, but they are really better suited to larger quantities.

Steamer
I like to steam foods as they retain so much of their nutritional value, colour and texture. You can use a colander and a saucepan but I think a steamer is a worthwhile investment if you intend to prepare your own food regularly for you baby – and, indeed, for all the family. I recommend that you buy a 'stacked steamer' – one with several tiers – so that you can cook more than one item at one time.

Freezer equipment

If you cook and freeze baby food in small portions, it makes life much easier. It is a good idea to reserve at least one section of your freezer purely for the storage of baby food, so you don't lose any tiny items. Buy plenty of ice-cube trays – these will be perfect to store single feed-sized portions of food. You can buy small pots specially designed for freezers, to hold larger quantities but empty yoghurt pots are a cheaper option. Do clean them thoroughly and sterilise them before use.

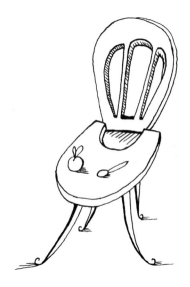

Food hygiene

Food hygiene is mainly a matter of common sense, but it is particularly important when there are babies and small children in the family, as they have immature immune systems. Keep your kitchen clean and, in the first few months of your baby's life, be scrupulous about sterilising bottles and feeding equipment and take extra care with the preparation and storage of the baby's food.

Basic hygiene rules

- Wash your hands with hot water and soap before preparing food and wash your children's hands before they start eating.
- Wash your hands after handling raw foods.
- Keep your kitchen surfaces and chopping boards clean.
- Wash cloths well in hot, soapy water.
- Use a dishwasher for kitchen equipment and pans, if you have one, as they wash at a high temperature. If not, wear rubber gloves so that you can wash equipment in very hot, soapy water, then rinse in clean, hot water and leave to drain, or dry on a clean tea towel (dish cloth).
- Sterilise bottles and teats until your baby is at least a year old. Sterilise other feeding equipment until he is feeding himself (see page 28).
- Always wash and dry fresh fruit and vegetables before you prepare them.
- Don't lick your fingers while preparing food and don't put tasting spoons back into food.

Storing food safely

- Once cooked, cool food as quickly as possible. This is best done by putting the covered pan into a sink with enough iced water to come halfway up the sides. As soon as it is completely cold, wrap appropriately and refrigerate or freeze.
- Do not leave cold food out of the fridge as bacteria can multiply rapidly at room temperature.
- Keep all perishable foods wrapped separately.
- Store raw and cooked foods separately. Raw meat should be well wrapped and stored at the bottom of the fridge so that it cannot drip on to other foods.
- Don't put warm food in the fridge and do not overfill the fridge or it will be more difficult to maintain the right temperature.
- Throw away any leftover food from your baby's plate. This may seem wasteful, but the saliva introduced from his spoon may help breed bacteria very quickly.
- Reheat food only once and make sure that it is hot right through to help kill off any bacteria.

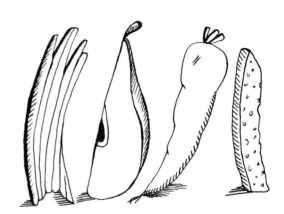

Sterilising equipment

As warm milk is the perfect breeding ground for bacteria, it is essential to sterilise all bottles, teats and feeding cups for the first year of your baby's life. It is best to sterilise all equipment until baby is are six months old. There are several types of steriliser.

Pot of boiling water
The simplest and cheapest way to sterilise things is in a big pan of boiling water. Just put everything into large saucepan and cover completely with water, bring to the boil, then boil for 10–15 minutes.

Steam steriliser
Steam sterilisers work in the same way but are quicker than traditional pot boiling, easy to use and just as effective.

Cold-water steriliser
This is simply a large plastic container into which you put all your equipment. You then cover with water, add a sterilising tablet and put on the lid, which comprises a grid to hold the utensils below the water. The water and tablet must be changed every day but this is a very safe, simple and convenient option.

Notes on the recipes

- Do not mix metric, imperial and American measures. Follow one set only.
- American terms are given in brackets.
- The ingredients are listed in the order in which they are used in the recipe.
- All spoon measurements are level:
  1 tsp = 15 ml; 1 tbsp = 15 ml.
- Eggs are medium unless otherwise stated. If you use a different size, adjust the amount of liquid added to obtain the right consistency.
- Can and packet sizes are approximate and will depend on the particular brand.
- Always wash, peel, core and seed, if necessary, fresh foods before use. Ensure that all produce is as fresh as possible and in good condition.

- Always use fresh herbs unless dried are specifically called for. If it is necessary to use dried herbs, use half the quantity stated. Chopped frozen varieties are much better than dried.
- Use whichever kitchen gadgets you like to speed up preparation and cooking times: mixers for whisking, food processors for grating, slicing, mixing or kneading, blenders for liquidising.
- All ovens vary, so cooking times have to be approximate. Adjust cooking times and temperatures according to manufacturer's instructions.
- Always preheat a conventional oven and cook on the centre shelf unless otherwise specified. Fan ovens do not require preheating.

You will notice that in the recipes in this book I have suggested specific unprocessed foods wherever possible. These include unrefined sugar; non-hydrogenated margarine; natural vanilla essence (extract); unsulphured apricots; sea salt; unrefined sunflower and sesame oil, etc. All of these products are easily available in health food stores and many large supermarkets stock some of them too. You can, of course, use your usual products – the choice is yours.

the earliest foods

4–6 months

Weaning and feeding your baby from liquids to solid foods is an exciting time. For this first stage, remember that your baby has only ever experienced one taste and one liquid texture – milk – so it's quite a culture shock to be presented with something new. You therefore need to move very slowly and gently so that the baby can happily progress at his own pace. Only the subtlest of changes – a thicker liquid, a little flavour – is all that is needed to start with.

It is important that you carry on feeding your baby breast or formula milk until six months, as suggested by current UK Government advice, since this will still constitute the main source of all his nutritional requirements. When you start your baby on solids, you will also be incorporating breast or formula milk into the soft purées.

Don't be too eager to introduce new flavours to your baby when you start him on solid foods. Your baby's tender taste buds will be happiest if you allow them to become accustomed to the taste of one single new food at a time and you will also be able to identify any adverse reactions as well as foods that they simply don't like. If your baby has an adverse reaction or rejects anything, make a note of the reaction and the item, then leave it off the menu for a while. You can try introducing it again a couple of weeks later.

Once your baby has become used to a small selection of foods, you may want to start making up combinations of ingredients that go well together, such as apple and pear, which will begin to lead you on to the next stage.

Foods you can introduce at four months
- Baby rice
- Cooked apple, papaya (pawpaw) and pear; ripe banana
- Cooked carrot, courgette (zucchini), marrow (squash), parsnip, potato, squash, swede (rutabaga)

Foods you can introduce at five months
- Non-wheat cereals, such as barley, oats and rye
- Cooked kiwi fruit, melon and plums
- Well-cooked lentils and other pulses
- Cooked spinach, celery, peas, leeks, sweetcorn (corn), cabbage, mushrooms, cauliflower and broccoli
- Soya

Baby rice purée

Baby rice is universally agreed to be the best first food to introduce. It is an extremely versatile ingredient and can be used as a meal on its own or to thicken other foods. A good tip is to feed your baby half his usual milk feed first, then offer the baby rice, followed by the rest of the milk.

NOT SUITABLE FOR FREEZING

MAKES 1 FEED

10 ml/2 tsp baby rice

15 ml/1 tbsp breast or formula milk

1 Put the baby rice into a sterilised small bowl, then gradually add the milk. Mix until you form a completely smooth and runny mixture.

2 The food should be served just lukewarm, so you can mix it in a small bowl standing in a bowl of hot water, or warm it gently in a pan or in the microwave. Stir it well and test the temperature before serving.

BEST FOR BABY Baby rice is specially formulated rice with a fine texture and is usually fortified with minerals and iron.

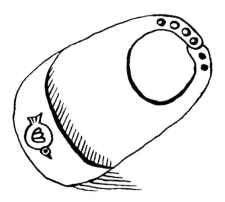

Avocado cream

Avocado cream is a perfect food for babies and generally very popular. Avocados are packed full of energy and high in nutritional value. Once cut, avocados do not keep well and cannot be frozen, so when you've fed one half to your baby, treat yourself to the other half!

NOT SUITABLE FOR FREEZING

MAKES 2 FEEDS

½ **ripe avocado**

15–30 ml/1–2 tbsp breast
or formula milk

1 Peel the avocado and remove the stone (pit) if necessary. Dice into small pieces and place in a small mixing bowl.

2 Mash the avocado using a fork and then mix in a little of the breast or formula milk until you have the consistency you want.

3 Tip into your baby's dish and serve cold.

Hints and variations If any of your purées are too thin, stir in a pinch of baby rice to thicken them slightly.

BEST FOR BABY Avocados are known to be a great brain food. This is because one of the many nutrients they contain is lecithin, which is essential for proper brain function – perfect for helping your baby to pass his school exams later in life!

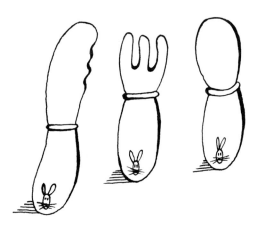

Baby mash

Because potatoes have such a mild flavour they make an excellent weaning food. If you are going to make potato mash for a tiny baby, you do need to pass it through a sieve. Don't use a food processor – it will break up the delicate starches in the potato and make it a stodgy mess.

NOT SUITABLE FOR FREEZING

MAKES 6 FEEDS

250 g/9 oz floury potatoes, peeled and cut into small dice

200 ml/7 fl oz/scant 1 cup breast or formula milk

1 Place the potatoes in a heavy-based saucepan and add just enough water to cover.

2 Bring to the boil, then reduce the heat, cover with a lid and simmer for 15–20 minutes until the potatoes are really tender.

3 Drain through a sieve (strainer) and then return to the pan.

4 Break down the potatoes with a masher and gradually add the milk until you have a creamy consistency, then use the back of a ladle to press the mixture through a fine sieve.

5 Turn into the baby's dish and serve warm.

Hints and variations Desirée is an excellent variety of floury potato that makes really good mash. The mash can be kept in the fridge for a couple of days.

BEST FOR BABY Introduce puréed vegetables individually. This helps the babies to develop their own understanding of taste and to distinguish the flavours of different foods.

Creamy carrot purée

Carrots have a naturally sweet flavour that babies enjoy and the bright colour introduces a different element to your baby's early food experiences. Adding breast or formula milk to the food not only helps produce a creamy taste and consistency, it also helps the process of weaning from milk to solid foods.

SUITABLE FOR FREEZING

MAKES 6 FEEDS

250 g/9 oz carrots, peeled and thinly sliced

250 ml/8 fl oz/1 cup breast or formula milk

1 Place the carrots in the basket of a steamer or in a metal colander set over a pan of boiling water.

2 Cover and cook for 15–18 minutes or until the carrots are really soft.

3 Liquidise the carrots in a small blender, then add the breast or formula milk until you have the consistency you want.

4 Tip into your baby's dish and serve warm.

Hints and variations You can use cooled, boiled water instead of milk if you prefer.

BEST FOR BABY It is a good idea to introduce a sweet vegetable to your baby's palate before a sweet fruit. It may help them to recognise and distinguish the many levels of sweetness.

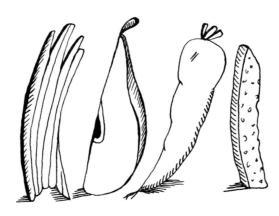

Sweet potato purée

Sweet potato is an incredible vegetable. There is a white variety, which is less nutritious, but the orange sweet potato is the most widely available. It has a vibrant colour, a slightly sweet taste and cooks more quickly than standard potato, making it a perfect first food for your baby.

SUITABLE FOR FREEZING

MAKES 4–6 FEEDS

250 g/9 oz sweet potatoes (about 2–3), peeled and cut into small dice

250 ml/8 fl oz/1 cup breast or formula milk

1 Place the potatoes in a heavy-based saucepan and cover with water.

2 Bring to the boil, then reduce the heat, cover and simmer for 12–15 minutes until the potatoes are tender.

3 Drain through a sieve (strainer), then return to the pan.

4 Break down the potatoes with a masher, then slowly add the milk until you have a creamy consistency.

5 Tip into your baby's dish and serve warm.

Hints and variations The ingredients will cool down as you purée them, so they should be just about at the right temperature to feed the baby once they have been prepared.

BEST FOR BABY Sweet potatoes are an excellent source of vitamin E, which is necessary for skin and brain development in young babies and throughout childhood.

Squidgy butternut squash

Butternut squash is, in my opinion, a very underrated vegetable that deserves to be more popular. It has a wonderful golden colour and sweet taste, it's widely available to buy in greengroceries and supermarkets and is very nutritious for your baby – and the whole family – to enjoy.

SUITABLE FOR FREEZING

MAKES 4–6 FEEDS

250 g/9 oz butternut squash, peeled, seeded and diced

Water

1 Place the diced squash in a heavy-based saucepan and add just enough water to cover.

2 Bring to the boil, then reduce the heat, cover and simmer over a low heat for 20 minutes until the squash is tender.

3 Drain through a sieve (strainer), reserving the cooking liquid.

4 Place the squash in a blender and add 30 ml/2 tbsp of the cooking liquid. Purée to a smooth pulp, adding a little more cooking liquid if necessary to obtain the right consistency for your baby.

5 Tip into your baby's dish and serve warm.

6 Divide the remainder into individual portions, then cool and freeze.

Hints and variations The outside of a squash is very tough, so use a serrated knife to dice it. You will also need a firm chopping board and cloth to steady the vegetable as you cut it.

BEST FOR BABY Butternut squash is a rich source of beta-carotene, a vitamin that is essential for building and maintaining healthy skin, respiratory system and vision.

Broccoli purée

Broccoli is one of the best green vegetables to introduce to babies of 4–6 months old, since it does not have the slightly off-putting bitterness that other green vegetables do. Its flavour is quite strong, but it is softened by the creaminess of the baby rice and milk in this recipe.

SUITABLE FOR FREEZING

MAKES 6 FEEDS

250 g/9 oz broccoli florets

10 ml/2 tsp baby rice

15 ml/1 tbsp breast or formula milk

1 Cut the broccoli into small pieces, then place in the basket of a steamer or a colander over a pan of boiling water.

2 Cover and steam for 10–12 minutes or until fully cooked.

3 Place in a blender and add the baby rice and milk. Liquidise for about 20 seconds until the mixture is smooth. You can add a little more breast or formula milk to thin the pulp down further if you wish.

4 Tip into your baby's dish and serve warm.

BEST FOR BABY It is always best to steam broccoli and for the shortest time possible. This is because it is full of vitamin C, which is destroyed on contact with water. Vitamin C is an antioxidant and therefore helps combat viral and bacterial infections.

Simple apple purée

All babies love apple – somehow children never seem to tire of its taste. It is also a most versatile fruit to use as a base for your recipes when you start creating more adventurous purées. Make sure you use sweet apples, however, and don't ever be tempted to add sugar.

SUITABLE FOR FREEZING

MAKES 6–8 FEEDS

2 eating (dessert) apples

30 ml/2 tbsp breast or formula milk

10 ml/2 tsp baby rice

1 Peel, core and dice the apples, place in a heavy-based saucepan and add a little water.

2 Cover, bring to the boil, then reduce the heat and simmer gently for 10 minutes until soft.

3 Strain the apples, reserving any cooking liquid, and place them in a blender. Add the milk and rice and liquidise to a smooth purée. Thin the purée if necessary with a little of the reserved cooking liquid.

4 Tip into your baby's dish and serve warm or cold.

Hints and variations I like to use Braeburn apples – they have plenty of flavour and cook well.

BEST FOR BABY Apples are rich in complex carbohydrates, which help maintain a steady level of glucose in the bloodstream and provide the energy and nutrients that your baby needs.

Magical mango fruit salad

By choosing two fruits that you think will blend well, adding breast or formula milk and a little baby rice, you can produce a very creamy and delicious fruit salad. Avoid using overpowering and acidic fruit, such as oranges, as these will be too strong for your baby's sensitive tastes at this stage.

SUITABLE FOR FREEZING

MAKES 6–8 FEEDS

½ **ripe mango**

1 **ripe pear**

10 ml/2 tsp **baby rice**

30 ml/2 tbsp **breast or formula milk**

1 Peel both fruit. Remove the stone (pit) from the mango if necessary and core the pear.

2 Chop the flesh into rough dice. Place in a steamer basket or in a metal colander over a pan of water.

3 Cover and steam the fruit for about 10 minutes until soft.

4 Transfer the fruit to a blender and add the baby rice and milk. Liquidise until the mixture becomes a creamy purée.

5 Tip into your baby's dish and serve warm or cold.

Hints and variations Try replacing the mango with papaya (pawpaw) and the pear with banana to make some different and interesting fruit combinations.

BEST FOR BABY Whilst introducing solids to your baby, it is very important to keep breast or formula milk as the main feed until he is at least six months. This recipe is an excellent example of how you can mix milk whilst still introducing solid food.

Soft papaya purée

Papaya is a tropical fruit that is readily available in major supermarkets. Their flesh, which has a fabulous rich orange colour, is sweet, juicy and refreshing. They don't need any cooking if fully ripe, so they make an instant feed for your young baby to enjoy either cold or warmed a little if you prefer.

SUITABLE FOR FREEZING

MAKES 4–6 FEEDS

1 very ripe papaya (pawpaw)

10 ml/2 tsp baby rice

1 Use a potato peeler to remove the outside skin of the papaya, then cut the fruit in half and scoop out and discard the black seeds. Chop the papaya flesh and place in a blender with the baby rice.

2 Blend until the mixture is smooth. You can add a little breast or formula milk to thin the pulp down further if you wish.

3 Tip into your baby's dish and serve just as it is.

BEST FOR BABY Raw fruit that is not fully ripe should not be given to young babies as it will upset their digestion. To check if a papaya, mango or avocado is ripe, simply press the outside of the fruit lightly. If the surface resists your pressure, then the fruit is not ripe. If it feels slightly soft to the touch, then it is perfect.

Pear purée

Pears have a refreshing and pleasant taste and a soft consistency that is easy for a young baby to eat and digest but they should be served cooked if your little one is under 5 months. Like apples, they have plenty of natural sweetness and so you should never be tempted to add sugar.

NOT SUITABLE FOR FREEZING

MAKES 6 FEEDS

1–2 ripe pears

200 ml/7 fl oz/scant 1 cup apple juice

10 ml/2 tsp baby rice

1 Peel, core and quarter the pears, then place the flesh in a saucepan and pour in the apple juice.

2 Cover with a lid and bring to the boil. Reduce the heat and simmer gently for 4–5 minutes.

3 Leave to cool a little in the pan, then add the baby rice and mash the ingredients together until you have the consistency you want. Alternatively you can purée the mixture in a blender.

4 Tip into your baby's dish and serve warm or cold.

Hints and variations Williams pears are a good choice for babies, having a soft consistency and sweet taste.

___

BEST FOR BABY Pears are rich in soluble fibre, which helps to maintain the digestive tract and lower blood cholesterol.

Pulped banana

Bananas don't freeze well, but since they make a perfect instant food, it really wouldn't be worth the trouble anyway! Highly nutritious, easy to prepare and packed in their own stay-fresh wrapper, they are the ideal fast food for your baby. No need to heat either – they taste delicious just as they are.

NOT SUITABLE FOR FREEZING

MAKES 2–3 FEEDS

1 ripe banana

10 ml/2 tsp baby rice

15 ml/1 tbsp breast or formula milk

1 Peel and slice the banana, then blend the flesh to a purée in a blender.

2 Mix the baby rice with the milk to form into a smooth mixture, then add it to the banana and blend until smooth.

3 Tip into your baby's dish and serve immediately.

Hints and variations Anything made with banana will start to discolour soon after making. If you have more than you need, cover it tightly with clingfilm (plastic wrap) and place in the fridge; it will last the rest of the day. However, since bananas are also good for you, I suggest you purée just enough for the baby and eat the rest!

BEST FOR BABY Recent research suggests that bananas may actually improve the quality of your sleep. This is because they help to stimulate the production of serotonin, the hormone that affects our moods. Could this help your baby sleep peacefully through the night? It's worth a try!

feeding inquisitive babies:

6–9 months

By the time your baby is around six months old, you will have experimented with a few basic flavours and perhaps begun to mix and match some more interesting dishes. You will also be around the stage of introducing a bit more texture, making your baby's purées less liquid and with a bit more body. You can also start to offer more fruits uncooked, simply preparing them, then grating or mashing them so your baby can manage them easily. You can also add a little more flavour with a few mildly flavoured herbs.

Remember, though, to be guided by your baby. If he is not ready for small, soft lumps or more adventurous flavours, he simply won't eat them. Stick with soft purées or familiar flavours for another week or so, then try again. Above all, remember that mealtimes should be a pleasure for both of you, and trying to encourage your baby to eat something he really doesn't want will only cause problems.

Although you can now start to introduce cows' milk in cooking (full-fat, not semi-skimmed or skimmed), it is important to continue giving your baby breast or formula milk to drink at this stage. This is because they both contain nutrients that are not found in cows' milk, such as iron and vitamin D.

Your baby is usually born with sufficient iron reserves to last for the first six months of his life but after this time iron-rich foods become important. For this reason, follow-on milk formulas are fortified with iron. However, these are hard to digest, so are best not used before six months.

Feeding himself

This is the part that some parents can't wait to get to – and others dread! There's no getting away from it, it is messy, but if you think about the co-ordination skills your baby needs to learn to get a spoonful of mushy food into his mouth, you should be impressed, not put off! Take the necessary precautions – a very large bib and some newspaper on the floor – and let the baby enjoy himself. Try not to get stressed – you don't want him to start to associate mealtimes with an unhappy atmosphere. Also, allow a little extra time for meals – and for clearing up afterwards.

The baby may start by trying to take the spoon from you, or putting his fingers in the bowl. Don't discourage him. Give him a second spoon to hold while you feed him – even if in the beginning not much will get from his spoon into his mouth! – and, if you can, choose foods that stick to the spoon rather than sliding off. Banana and porridge are particularly good. As he begins to master handling his spoon, you can have two spoons on the go: you put a little food on to the end of one spoon, then give it to him to feed himself while you recharge the second one.

You can also introduce some finger foods for the baby to suck: rusks, pieces of lightly cooked vegetable or breadsticks make a good start.

Foods you can introduce at six months

- Cows' milk products in cooking: this includes mild cheese, yoghurt and fromage frais; all should be made from pasteurised full-fat milk – low-fat varieties do not contain all the nutrients needed by a growing baby
- Soaked dried fruit, such as apricots and peaches but not raisins and sultanas (golden raisins)
- White fish, such as cod, plaice and haddock
- Strawberries and tomatoes
- Chicken and turkey – white meat (breast) only
- Tofu; cocoa (unsweetened chocolate) powder
- Unsweetened diluted fruit juices, such as apple and orange (see page 17)

Foods you can introduce at seven months

In addition to the foods you have been giving your baby, you can now start introduce the following foods to add more variety to your baby's diet.
- Bread, breadsticks, rusks, crispbread, pasta
- Cooked egg yolk (but not the white)
- More varieties of fruit, including citrus fruit and berry fruits, such as satsumas (peeled and all pips and membranes removed), strawberries and raspberries
- Lean red meat, such as beef and lamb
- Well-cooked lentils and other pulses
- Fingers of cooked vegetables, such as carrot, butternut squash or sweet potato

Foods you can introduce at nine months

Once your baby is happy with the foods you introduced at seven months, you can add even more to the range.
- Cooked whole eggs
- Oily and canned fish, such as sardines, mackerel, salmon and tuna
- Soaked raisins and sultanas (golden raisins)
- Finely ground nuts but not peanuts (see Allergies and intolerances, page 23)
- Sticks of raw fruit and vegetables, such as mango, pineapple, peppers and baby sweetcorn (corn)

Foods to avoid

There is still a long list of foods that are not suitable, no matter how eager your baby is to try them! The following should not be given to your baby yet.

- Coffee, tea and fizzy drinks
- Fruit juices and squashes that contain sugar
- High-fibre foods, such as muesli and whole grains
- Honey
- Low-fat dairy products, such as cheeses and yoghurts
- Whole nuts
- Salt, stock cubes and hot spices
- Shellfish

Salmon and fresh mint pâté

Canned red salmon is wonderfully useful and it's a good idea to keep a couple of cans on hand in the storecupboard for whenever you need them. The texture of this pâté is quite soft, but you can adjust it by blending for more or less time to make it as coarse as your baby likes it.

SUITABLE FOR FREEZING

MAKES 4–6 BABY PORTIONS

5 ml/1 tsp coarsely chopped fresh mint leaves

100 g/4 oz canned red salmon, drained and all bones removed

45 ml/3 tbsp full-fat plain Greek yoghurt

10 ml/2 tsp tomato purée (paste)

5 ml/1 tsp lemon juice

1 Place the mint leaves in a blender and blend until the herb is completely broken down.

2 Add the salmon, yoghurt, tomato purée and lemon juice. Blend the mixture until it turns to a smooth and light consistency.

Hints and variations Try using other canned oily fish, such as mackerel, pilchards or sardines. All of these are delicious and perfect for young babies – but do take great care to remove all the bones.

BEST FOR BABY Salmon is rich in the essential fatty acid, omega 3, which is believed to help with the development of the brain and its correct function – so it's of great benefit for young babies' brains.

make meals a happy and relaxed time from the start

offer children healthy options – and make them more fun

Avocado and tomato dip

This recipe makes an interesting and flavoursome dip. It's a great idea to combine half avocado and half peas, as avocado on its own has an extremely rich taste. Also your baby may be cutting his first teeth, so serving crispy pieces of bread or savoury bread fingers would complement this dip well.

NOT SUITABLE FOR FREEZING

MAKES 4–6 BABY PORTIONS

1 spring onion (scallion), roughly chopped

½ ripe avocado, peeled, stoned (pitted) and roughly chopped

2 ripe tomatoes, roughly chopped

15 ml/1 tbsp peas, thawed if frozen

2.5 ml/½ tsp ground cumin

15 ml/1 tbsp chopped coriander (cilantro) leaves

Juice of ½ lemon

5 ml/1 tsp full-fat plain live yoghurt (optional)

Fingers of wholemeal bread or toast

1 Place the spring onion in a blender and blend until finely chopped.

2 Add the avocado, tomatoes, peas, cumin and coriander and blend to a smooth purée.

3 Add the lemon juice and blend for a few seconds to mix the ingredients thoroughly.

4 Turn into a serving dish, garnish with a spoonful of yoghurt, if liked, and serve with fingers of wholemeal bread or toast.

BEST FOR BABY Dips such as this are great for encouraging babies to feed themselves. You can regulate the texture of a dip very easily by making it thicker and coarser to encourage chewing.

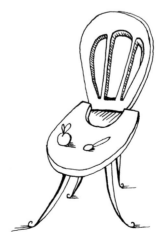

Thick vegetable soup

Thick puréed soups such as this one are perfect to feed babies under one year old but, of course, they provide lots of goodness for children of any age. And, provided that they are served in sturdy baby bowls, soups are another great way of encouraging self-feeding.

SUITABLE FOR FREEZING

MAKES 8–10 BABY PORTIONS

2 large or 3–4 medium leeks

50 g/2 oz/¼ cup butter

2 medium potatoes, peeled and cut into small dice

1 medium onion, peeled and finely chopped

1 garlic clove, peeled and crushed

10 ml/2 tsp dried chives or 1 small bunch of fresh chives

1 litre/1¾ pts/4¼ cups vegetable stock

500 ml/17 fl oz/2¼ cups full-fat milk

Bread

1 Trim off the tops and roots of the leeks and discard the tough outer layer. Split the leeks in half lengthways and slice them quite finely.

2 Wash the leeks thoroughly in water and drain well.

3 In a large heavy-based saucepan, gently melt the butter and add the potatoes and onion. Sauté for 2 minutes until softened and transparent, then add the garlic. If you are using dried chives, add them now. (Fresh chives should be added later.)

4 Add the leeks. Allow all of the ingredients to sweat very gently over a low heat for 10 minutes, stirring occasionally.

5 Add the stock and milk and bring to the boil. Turn the heat down to a gentle simmer and cook for a further 10 minutes.

6 Meanwhile, warm your bread in the oven. If you are using fresh chives, chop them as finely as possible.

7 Tip the soup into a food processor or hand blender and liquidise, if liked, then pour a portion into your baby's bowl.

8 Stir in the chopped fresh chives, if using, and serve with warm bread.

BEST FOR BABY Healthy plants contain substances that help protect against disease and environmental stress. Clearly, the more natural vitality our food has, the more will be passed on to our bodies as we eat.

Tomato and red pepper soup

This raw vegetable soup is one of the best things you could possibly feed your little one. The recipe is very simple and provides a great way of using up soft and over-ripe tomatoes. In fact, you'll find that the softer the tomato, the sweeter and richer the taste of the soup.

NOT SUITABLE FOR FREEZING

MAKES 8 BABY PORTIONS

4 ripe tomatoes

½ cucumber

2 spring onions (scallions)

1 red (bell) pepper

10 ml/2 tsp unrefined caster (superfine) sugar

15 ml/1 tbsp tomato purée (paste)

30 ml/2 tbsp good-quality virgin olive oil

100 ml/3½ fl oz/scant ½ cup water or full-fat milk

1 Wash all the vegetables and roughly chop them into small dice.

2 Place all the ingredients in a food processor or liquidiser and blend for a good minute or until you have a smooth consistency. The dish is then ready to serve.

Serving suggestions Although this recipe makes a soup, it can also be used as a basic tomato sauce that you can use to make family favourites such as spaghetti with cheese and tomato, or in a delicious bolognaise sauce.

BEST FOR BABY Cucumber is thought to help to improve calcium absorption and therefore help growing teeth and bones, and research has shown that it also strengthens the heart and nerve tissue – so it's a brilliant choice for your baby. Cucumber also contains the digestive enzyme erepsis, which may help to clean the intestines.

Cottage cheese with papaya

Always use full-fat cottage cheese if your baby is under one year old – low-fat dairy products are not suitable for him yet. The papaya pulp makes an interesting taste combination and is ideal for encouraging self-feeding. You can also spread it on baby rice cakes or savoury fingers.

NOT SUITABLE FOR FREEZING

MAKES 4 BABY PORTIONS

1 ripe papaya (pawpaw)

50 g/2 oz/¼ cup full-fat cottage cheese

10 ml/2 tsp baby rice

1 Peel the papaya and remove and discard the seeds.

2 Place the flesh in a blender with the cottage cheese and baby rice. Liquidise for 10–15 seconds to break down and combine the ingredients lightly.

3 Tip into your baby's bowl and serve.

Hints and variations This meal will keep successfully, covered, in the fridge for up to two days.

BEST FOR BABY Papayas are rich in papain (a protein-digesting enzyme) and may help to balance the natural juices in a baby's developing stomach. This, in turn, will aid digestion in these early stages of eating solid foods.

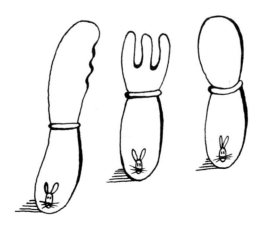

Carrot and broccoli mash with cheese

Carrots and broccoli make a delicious combination and by adding a little potato and some grated cheese you can create a tasty and nutritious meal for your inquisitive baby to enjoy. As an alternative to the milk in this recipe, you can use any vegetable cooking water you may have to hand.

SUITABLE FOR FREEZING

MAKES 6–8 BABY PORTIONS

250 g/9 oz potato, peeled and cut into small dice

2 medium carrots, peeled and cut into small dice

150 g/5 oz broccoli florets

50 g/2 oz grated full-fat Cheddar cheese

200 ml/7 fl oz/scant 1 cup full-fat milk

1 Place the diced potato and carrots in a steamer and cook for 8 minutes. Add the broccoli florets and continue to cook for a further 8 minutes or until soft.

2 Add the cheese and milk and blend with the vegetables.

3 Tip into your baby's bowl and serve warm.

Hints and variations You can use sweet potato instead of an ordinary variety – they can be cooked for the same time and will also help enhance the colour and taste of the final dish.

BEST FOR BABY Broccoli is extremely rich in zinc, a mineral that is needed for the production of red blood cells. It also contains sulfaphane, a plant chemical believed to trigger the body's production of enzymes that guard against damage to the DNA in cells.

Couscous pilaff

This brightly coloured dish is packed full of iron and protein. It also contains extra-virgin olive oil, which is made from the first pressing of olives and has a delicious aromatic taste. If your baby finds it too strong, simply substitute plain olive oil, which is much lighter and milder.

SUITABLE FOR FREEZING

MAKES 6–8 BABY PORTIONS

50 g/2 oz/½ cup couscous

2.5 ml/½ tsp ground turmeric

150 ml/¼ pt/⅔ cup fresh
vegetable stock

15 ml/1 tbsp canned lentils

½ red (bell) pepper, roughly chopped

½ yellow pepper, roughly chopped

15 ml/1 tbsp peas, thawed if frozen

Juice of ½ lemon

15 ml/1 tbsp extra-virgin olive oil

1 Place a medium-sized frying pan (skillet) over a high heat and add the couscous granules and turmeric. Allow the couscous to roast for 2–3 minutes until golden.

2 Pour in the vegetable stock and turn off the heat. Leave the couscous for a few minutes to absorb the stock.

3 Meanwhile, put the lentils and peppers in a blender and liquidise until finely chopped.

4 Add all the remaining ingredients, including the couscous, and mix together well.

5 Tip into your baby's dish and serve warm.

Hints and variations Proprietary stock cubes are not suitable for babies under 1 year old as they contain a lot of salt, so I use fresh home-made stock. Alternatively, you can use 2.5 ml/½ tsp of yeast extract, such as Vecon, diluted in 150 ml/¼ pt/⅔ cup of hot water.

When your baby is older, you can make this with chopped cooked chicken or fish, such as tuna, instead of lentils.

BEST FOR BABY Lentils – and other pulses – contain lots of protein, which is essential for building healthy bodies. Olive oil also contains many health-promoting nutrients but be sure to choose a top-quality brand.

Cheesy lentil and vegetable casserole

Casseroles provide a wonderful way for your baby to experience and enjoy many different ingredients, tastes and flavours, and a subtle means of introducing new foods to your baby. Try adding other vegetables too, such as aubergine, courgettes, etc. – but remember to do this one at a time.

SUITABLE FOR FREEZING

MAKES 8 BABY PORTIONS

25 g/1 oz/2 tbsp butter

½ medium onion, finely chopped

2.5 ml/½ tsp dried mixed herbs

2 leeks, trimmed, well washed and finely chopped

200 g/7 oz sweet potatoes, peeled and cut into small dice

50 g/2 oz/⅓ cup red lentils

1 celery stick, finely chopped

450 ml/¾ pt/2 cups water

1 bay leaf

50 g/2 oz/¼ cup grated full-fat cheese

1 Melt the butter in a large saucepan and add the onion and mixed herbs. Sauté for a couple of minutes to soften and then add the chopped leeks and continue to sauté for 1–2 minutes until soft.

2 Add the sweet potatoes, lentils and celery and sauté for 1 further minute.

3 Add the water and bring to the boil, then cover with a lid, reduce the heat and simmer for 25–35 minutes until all the vegetables are tender.

4 Remove the bay leaf and stir in the grated cheese.

5 Pour into a blender or food processor and liquidise to a texture suitable for your baby.

6 Tip into your baby's bowl and serve once it is cool enough to eat.

Hints and variations You can serve this dish to your baby at any age from 6 months, though by the time he is around 9 months, you should not need to purée it. Gradually make the chunks of vegetables slightly bigger as your baby grows so that he gets used to chewing.

BEST FOR BABY Whatever we are doing, our approach will contribute to the end result in a huge way. Try to be mindful of this as you prepare a meal, and stir in a little love as the dish takes shape.

Roasted root vegetable mash

Roasting vegetables such as carrots, parsnips and swede increases their sweetness while still retaining many of their vital nutrients. This is a great way to introduce the many levels of taste and sweetness that vegetables can provide and you can vary the combinations of ingredients according to what you have available.

SUITABLE FOR FREEZING

MAKES 8 BABY PORTIONS

150 g/5 oz parsnips, peeled

150 g/5 oz carrots, peeled

150 g/5 oz swede (rutabaga)

10 ml/2 tsp dried parsley

2.5 ml/½ tsp ground turmeric

30 ml/2 tbsp extra-virgin olive oil

100 ml/3½ fl oz/scant ½ cup water

1 Preheat the oven to 200°C/400°F/gas 6/fan oven 180°C.

2 Cut all the vegetables into very small dice and lay them on a baking (cookie) sheet. Sprinkle over the parsley, turmeric and olive oil and then place in the oven. Roast for 20 minutes.

3 After this time, stir the vegetables to make sure that they are cooked evenly on all sides and return to the oven for 5 minutes to finish.

4 Remove the vegetables from the oven and place in a food processor or blender, with enough of the water to make a soft purée. Adjust the texture according to you baby's chewing ability.

5 Tip into your baby's bowl and serve warm.

BEST FOR BABY The first solid foods given to your child will determine later eating habits. Foods laden with sweeteners, oil or salt will encourage cravings for these foods as baby develops.

Leek and pea purée with cumin

Leeks and peas are a classic marriage of flavours and the addition of cumin gives a wonderful exotic taste to this purée. Peas have a tendency to produce wind but I was once told that the addition of cumin or oregano helps prevent this. For me, it does seem to work and it certainly tastes delicious!

SUITABLE FOR FREEZING

MAKES 4–6 BABY PORTIONS

25 g/1 oz/2 tbsp butter

1 medium leek, trimmed, well washed and finely chopped

A pinch of dried oregano

A pinch of ground cumin

175 g/6 oz potato, peeled and cut into small dice

250 ml/8 fl oz/1 cup water

75 g/3 oz/¾ cup frozen peas

1 Melt the butter in a medium-sized saucepan and add the chopped leek, oregano and cumin.

2 Sauté gently until the leek is lightly golden, then add the diced potato and water. Bring to the boil, then reduce the heat and simmer for 10 minutes or until the potatoes are cooked.

3 Add the peas and continue to simmer for 5 minutes until tender.

4 Tip into a blender and purée until you achieve the desired consistency.

5 Tip into your baby's bowl and serve warm.

Hints and variations This purée can easily be made into a soup by adding more liquid. It is best to use mainly the white part of the leek, which is more tender and mildly flavoured.

BEST FOR BABY Peas are rich in chlorophyll, which has long been known as a blood-builder. Chlorophyll is the substance that makes plants appear green and so it is a really good idea to get your child accustomed to enjoying green foods.

Swede and nutmeg mash

Swedes make a lovely mash – a welcome change from the usual potato variety, which has a completely different texture. With grated nutmeg and just a little soft brown sugar to enhance its beautiful creamy sweet taste, this humble vegetable makes a colourful addition to any baby's plate.

SUITABLE FOR FREEZING

MAKES 8 BABY PORTIONS

500 g/18 oz swede (rutabaga), peeled and cut into small dice

25 g/1 oz/2 tbsp butter

100 ml/3½ fl oz/scant ½ cup full-fat milk

A small pinch of freshly grated nutmeg

10 ml/2 tsp unrefined soft brown sugar

1 Place the diced swede in large saucepan and cover with water. Bring to the boil, then reduce the heat and simmer for 18–20 minutes until tender.

2 Drain the swede, then put in a blender. Add the butter, milk, nutmeg and sugar and blend to the desired consistency.

3 Tip into your baby's bowl and serve warm.

Hints and variations You can try adding other spices – ground cinnamon, ground cardamom and ground ginger all work well. You can also use parsnip or sweet potato instead of the swede – the cooking time is the same.

BEST FOR BABY Do be sparing when adding herbs and spices. The idea is for them to be background flavours that are barely noticeable. This way your baby is more likely to accept them as you increase the intensity of their flavour.

Sautéed mushrooms with tarragon

There are many varieties of mushroom available for you to experiment with and all are perfectly suitable for young children and babies. However, some have a fairly strong taste and texture. Button mushrooms have the mildest flavour and are therefore the best to start with for a young baby's sensitive taste buds.

SUITABLE FOR FREEZING

MAKES 4–6 BABY PORTIONS

100 g/4 oz button mushrooms, wiped clean

2 spring onions (scallions), chopped

25 g/1 oz/2 tbsp butter

2.5 ml/½ tsp dried tarragon

10 ml/2 tsp cranberry sauce

30 ml/2 tbsp full-fat plain Greek yoghurt

25 g/1 oz/2 tbsp grated full-fat Cheddar cheese

1 Place the mushrooms and spring onions in a blender and liquidise until finely chopped.

2 Meanwhile, heat a frying pan (skillet) and add the butter. Once melted, add the chopped mushrooms and onion.

3 Place the tarragon in the food processor and blend until chopped.

4 Add to the mushroom mixture in the pan, together with the tarragon, cranberry sauce, cheese and yoghurt. Stir gently over a gentle heat, to incorporate all of the ingredients.

5 Turn off the heat and allow the mushrooms to cool.

6 Tip a portion into your baby's bowl and serve.

BEST FOR BABY Mushrooms are considered to be particularly helpful in clearing mucus either from the lungs or digestive tract so if your baby is a bit wheezy, you might like to try them on this recipe.

Tuna and chive delight

Fish is a really important food group, packed full of valuable nutrients, so try and include it in your baby's diet every week. Canned tuna makes a convenient fish to use but make sure you buy it in oil, not brine, as the latter contains too much salt. This gorgeous mousse is almost good enough to serve as a starter for a dinner party!

SUITABLE FOR FREEZING

MAKES 4 BABY PORTIONS

A small handful of fresh coriander (cilantro) leaves

85 g/3½ oz/very small can of tuna in sunflower oil, drained

10 ml/2 tsp tomato purée (paste)

10 ml/2 tsp dried chives

45 ml/3 tbsp full-fat plain Greek yoghurt

15 ml/1 tbsp pure baby rice

1 Coarsely chop the coriander leaves or snip them with a pair of scissors. Place in a blender and liquidise until the herb is completely broken down.

2 Add the flaked tuna, tomato purée, chives and yoghurt. Blend the mixture until it turns to a smooth and light consistency.

3 Add the baby rice and blend for 5 seconds.

4 Tip into your baby's bowl and serve just as it is.

BEST FOR BABY This is an excellent way of incorporating fresh herbs into your baby's food, so do experiment, using other herbs such as fresh basil. Just make sure that they are very well blended.

Sweet potato and lentil purée

Sweet potatoes are, in my opinion, a seriously under-used vegetable. They have a wonderful bright colour to them that babies find very attractive. When combined with the subtle flavour of the lentils, they make a delicious creamy purée that will keep in the fridge for up to two days.

SUITABLE FOR FREEZING

MAKES 8 BABY PORTIONS

1 sweet potato, about 200 g/7 oz

225 g/8 oz/medium can of lentils with no added salt

150 ml/¼ pt/⅔ cup full-fat plain set live yoghurt

30 ml/2 tbsp tomato purée (paste)

1 Peel and cut the sweet potato into small dice. Place in a saucepan and cover with water. Bring to the boil, then reduce the heat and simmer for 15–16 minutes or until soft.

2 Meanwhile, drain the canned lentils, then place them in a blender or food processor.

3 Once the potatoes are cooked, drain off the water, and add the potatoes to the lentils. Add the yoghurt and tomato purée. Blend until smooth.

4 Tip into your baby's bowl and serve warm.

Hints and variations Try adding some finely chopped fresh herbs to add a little variety or some grated cheese to enrich the purée.

BEST FOR BABY Make sure you buy pulses canned without salt – they are widely available. Alternatively, you could use cooked dried lentils, which are much cheaper. Place in a saucepan, cover with cold water and leave to soak for several hours, preferably overnight. Drain, then cover with fresh cold water. Do not add salt. Bring to the boil and cook for 18–20 minutes or until soft and tender, then drain and leave to cool completely. In this state they can be frozen for future use. Puy lentils do not need soaking, although if you do so the night before they will cook in half the given time.

Pear and apple pudding

Sweet ripe pears and apples make nutritious and ideal foods to introduce as new and exciting tastes to the youngest baby, and served together they give a really good balance of flavours. Combining them with a little baby rice not only provides a pleasant consistency and texture but also extra nutritional value.

SUITABLE FOR FREEZING

MAKES 4–6 BABY PORTIONS

1 eating (dessert) apple

1 ripe pear

30 ml/2 tbsp water

30 ml/2 tbsp baby rice

1 Peel, core and wash the apple and pear, then chop into small pieces.

2 Put the pieces of apple into a small heavy-based saucepan and add the measured water.

3 Cook over a low heat for about 4 minutes until tender. Add the pieces of pear, and cook for a few more minutes until both fruit are very soft.

4 Mix a little water with the baby rice to make into a purée, then add to the cooked fruit. Tip into a small blender and liquidise to a smooth purée.

5 Spoon a portion into your baby's bowl and cool until lukewarm, then serve.

BEST FOR BABY Babies over 6 months old can have raw fruit (see page 47), provided that the fruit is ripe and juicy in its raw state. Apples are rather hard and always tend to benefit from a little cooking, but pears, melon and plums can all be used raw to make purées.

getting chewy:

9–12 months

By this stage, you will be reducing the amount of breast or formula milk you give your baby. However, it is still important that he receives about 400 ml/14 fl oz/ 1¾ cups of full-fat milk a day, as the fat it contains is still a key nutrient at this age. As you increase the amount of solid food he eats, you can gradually reduce his breast or formula milk feeds. For most babies, the last feed to be dropped is the one just before they go to sleep, as this is a good way to relax and comfort them before they go down for the night.

Your baby will be learning to chew now, so you can gradually introduce more challenging foods to encourage him. Most vegetables and fruits can simply be finely chopped or sliced, and meat should be minced (ground) or very finely chopped.

This is a good time to introduce raw vegetables and salads. Research has suggested that if these foods are introduced to a baby, they are far more likely to be enjoyed in later life, providing the way to a balanced and healthy diet. It is important to lead by example, of course, so try to ensure that your whole family enjoys eating vegetables and salads as part of their regular diet.

Many babies are quite chubby at around 12 months, but this is quite normal. As long as they are receiving a well-balanced and nutritious diet and are growing well, there's nothing to worry about. Once they become mobile, especially when they start to walk, they will soon lose any extra fat. If you are at all concerned that your baby is gaining too much weight, however, speak to your health visitor or GP.

By now your baby will be eating all kinds of foods, including sweet and savoury 'treats'. There's nothing wrong with this as long as the treats form only a small part of a healthy balanced diet. But try not to introduce your baby to too many snacks with a high fat, salt or sugar content. While you are still able to control what he eats, you should try to ensure that he doesn't get a taste for these tempting but nutritionally unsound foods.

Your growing baby will now be joining in the family's normal eating routine. Instead of making meals specially for him, you will be able to start making the family meal by simply chopping up the baby's portion more finely – and making sure it is not too hot! You'll therefore find that in this chapter, I have started to offer serving suggestions and ideas that relate to the whole family and not just the baby.

Pasta is popular with all ages and so, on pages 67–70, I've included some of my favourite pasta sauce recipes, which are all suitable for babies from 9–12 months, and will be enjoyed by older children and adults too.

Foods you can introduce at 12 months

- Shellfish (see Allergies and intolerances, page 23)
- Honey
- Salt and spices - in small quantities
- Smooth peanut butter (see Allergies and intolerances, on page 23)
- Unsweetened fruit juices and squashes (see page 17)
- Wholewheat pasta and wholemeal bread (but not whole grains)

Button mushroom and Cheddar cheese dip

This mushroom dip can also double up as a pâté. It's a fabulous way of introducing mushrooms to babies; in fact this dip is so tasty that it can be served as a delicious light lunch, spread on buttered toast. Tarragon is the perfect herb to complement mushrooms and is readily available.

SUITABLE FOR FREEZING

**MAKES 8 BABY PORTIONS
OR 2 ADULT PORTIONS**

25 g/1 oz/2 tbsp butter

½ onion, peeled and chopped

400 g/14 oz button mushrooms,
wiped clean

10 ml/2 tsp cranberry sauce

50 ml/2 fl oz/3½ tbsp full-fat plain
Greek yoghurt

25 g/1 oz/2 tbsp grated full-fat
Cheddar cheese

15 ml/1 tbsp chopped fresh parsley

1 Heat a medium-sized frying pan (skillet), then add the butter and melt.

2 Add the onion and sauté gently.

3 While the onion is cooking, chop the mushrooms finely in a food processor if you have one.

4 Add these to the pan and continue to sauté gently for a couple of minutes.

5 Add the cranberry sauce, yoghurt and cheese and stir gently to incorporate all of the ingredients.

6 Leave the dip to cool – this will help to thicken it. Sprinkle with fresh parsley before serving.

Serving suggestions This mushroom dip is delicious with Cheesy Twigs (see page 86) or any suitable savoury baby biscuits (crackers).

Hints and variations You can also heat this dip and use it as a mushroom sauce to go with fish or chicken.

BEST FOR BABY Mushrooms are a good source of potassium, which is needed for the nerve and muscle functions that are vital to your baby's developing co-ordination skills.

Lentil and carrot dhal

Lentils are perfect to feed to hungry growing babies. They are packed full of nutrients. They combine particularly well with apple and this is the base to this slightly textured dhal. You can serve it to babies of 6 months if you wish, but you will need to blend the dish to a fine purée.

SUITABLE FOR FREEZING

MAKES 8 BABY PORTIONS

25 g/1 oz/2 tbsp butter

½ onion, peeled and finely chopped

A pinch of ground turmeric

A pinch of ground cumin

50 g/2 oz/⅓ cup red lentils

1 medium eating (dessert) apple, peeled and finely chopped

2 carrots, peeled and finely chopped

350 ml/12 fl oz/1⅓ cups vegetable stock

1 Heat the butter in a medium saucepan. Once it has melted, add the chopped onion and the spices. Cook for 1–2 minutes and then add the lentils, apple and carrots.

2 Continue to cook for 1–2 minutes, then add the vegetable stock. Bring to the boil, then reduce the heat and simmer for 10 minutes until the vegetables are very tender.

3 Mash with a potato masher.

4 Allow to cool, then serve.

Hints and variations Unlike other pulses, red lentils do not need soaking before cooking. However, it does speed up the cooking time if you do so.

BEST FOR BABY As well as being a rich source of iron, lentils may help to avoid those painful, windy tummies as they do not contain sulphur, a mineral that can cause wind, which is contained in other pulses.

Tomato sauce with garden herbs

When your baby is 9–12 months old, you can start to offer him well-cooked pasta. I recommend trying wholewheat varieties, rather than let him get a taste for the white refined type. Provided that it is well cooked (see page 68), it is delicious and also an extremely good source of beneficial fibre.

SUITABLE FOR FREEZING

MAKES ABOUT 500 ML/17 FL OZ/2¼ CUPS

15 ml/1 tbsp olive oil

1 medium onion, peeled and chopped

2.5 ml/½ tsp dried chives

2.5 ml/½ tsp dried rosemary

2.5 ml/½ tsp dried basil

225 g/8 oz/small can of chopped tomatoes

200 g/7 oz cherry tomatoes, roughly chopped

15 ml/1 tbsp tomato purée (paste)

10 ml/2 tsp unrefined caster (superfine) sugar

1 Heat the oil in a large saucepan over a medium heat. Add the onion and herbs and cook gently for 3–4 minutes.

2 Place the chopped tomatoes in a blender or food processor and blend for a few seconds to break them down.

3 Add to the pan of onion and herbs with the fresh tomatoes, tomato purée and sugar.

4 Bring to a boil, then reduce the heat and cook gently for 12–14 minutes until the sauce is thick and pulpy.

5 Serve warm with cooked pasta (see page 68).

Serving suggestions Grate some cheese over the top for extra taste.

Hints and variations This sauce makes a great base to favourites such as spaghetti bolognaise, lasagne and casseroles.

BEST FOR BABY Olive oil contains oleic acid, which is beneficial for many bodily functions.

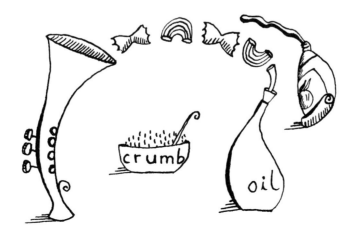

Ricotta with spinach and Parmesan sauce

When cooking pasta, allow about 25 g/1 oz for your baby and up to 75 g/3 oz per adult portion. Bring a large pan of lightly salted water to the boil, then gradually add the pasta. Bring back to the boil, then reduce the heat and simmer until the pasta is very tender. Wholewheat varieties will take 15–20 minutes, white varieties rather less.

SUITABLE FOR FREEZING

MAKES ABOUT 350 ML/12 FL OZ/1⅓ CUPS

15 ml/1 tbsp olive oil

1 medium onion, peeled and finely chopped

1 garlic clove, peeled and finely crushed

A pinch of grated nutmeg

50 g/2 oz thawed frozen spinach

100 g/4 oz/½ cup ricotta cheese

100 g/4 oz/1 cup finely grated Parmesan cheese

Juice of ½ lemon

1 Heat the oil in a large saucepan over a medium heat. Add the onion, garlic and nutmeg and cook gently for 2–3 minutes.

2 Chop the spinach roughly with a knife and then add to the onion mixture with the two cheeses.

3 Heat gently until the cheese have melted, then stir all of the ingredients together until thoroughly combined.

4 Remove from the heat and add lemon juice to taste.

5 Serve warm with cooked pasta.

Serving suggestions You can also use this sauce to make cauliflower cheese with a little 'twist', or as an extra-special lasagne topping.

BEST FOR BABY Even frozen spinach is packed full of important nutrients. One of these is chromium, a mineral that can help balance the blood sugar levels in the body. Another good source of chromium is sweetcorn (corn).

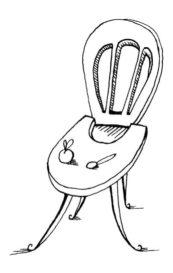

Roasted Provençal vegetable pasta sauce

This is a really versatile sauce, suitable for vegetarians, baby and adult. Roasting the vegetables first brings out their wonderful mellow flavour and the herbs add an extra special touch. You can, of course, vary the ingredients as your baby gets older, perhaps adding a diced aubergine.

SUITABLE FOR FREEZING

MAKES ABOUT 400 ML/4 FL OZ/1¾ CUPS

1 medium red onion, peeled and finely chopped

1 courgette (zucchini), finely chopped

1 red (bell) pepper, finely chopped

30 ml/2 tbsp olive oil

15 ml/1 tbsp tomato purée (paste)

10 ml/2 tsp dried Provençal herbs

5 ml/1 tsp unrefined caster (superfine) sugar

Freshly ground black pepper

225 g/8 oz/small can of tomatoes

1 Preheat the oven to 200°C/400°F/gas 6/fan oven 180°C.

2 Lay the chopped vegetables on a baking (cookie) tray. Mix the olive oil in a small bowl with the tomato purée, herbs, sugar and black pepper.

3 Pour the mixture over the diced vegetables and place in the oven to bake for 14–16 minutes, turning the vegetables over once or twice, until they are all tender and lightly browned.

4 Transfer to a food processor, add the canned tomatoes and blend, using the pulse facility to control the texture. If the sauce is a little too thick, add a little water to thin it slightly.

5 Serve warm over freshly boiled pasta (see page 68).

Serving suggestions This is delicious served with grated Mozzarella or even Parmesan cheese. The flavour of Parmesan is quite strong, but it is surprising how willing young babies who enjoy their food are to try new foods.

Hints and variations Use this Provençal sauce to make a roasted vegetable lasagne for a change.

BEST FOR BABY By this time, your baby's food should have enough 'bits' in it to encourage him to chew. To avoid turning everything into a mush when blending, it is a good idea to use the pulse facility of your food processor to control the texture.

Creamy mushroom and ham sauce

This wonderful sauce will be a favourite with all the family. As well as making a delicious meal with pasta, it can be served over cooked new potatoes, or used to stuff savoury crêpes. You could also pile it into a simple crisp jacket potato to make a delicious vegetarian meal.

SUITABLE FOR FREEZING

MAKES ABOUT 500 ML/17 FL OZ/2¼ CUPS

15 ml/1 tbsp unrefined sunflower oil

1 medium onion, peeled and finely chopped

50 g/2 oz cooked sliced ham, shredded

1 garlic clove, peeled and crushed

15 ml/1 tbsp chopped fresh parsley

25 g/1 oz/2 tbsp butter

100 g/4 oz button mushrooms, thinly sliced

200 ml/7 fl oz/scant 1 cup double (heavy) cream

1 Heat the sunflower oil in a large saucepan. Add the onion and sauté for 2–3 minutes to soften slightly.

2 Add the shredded ham, together with the garlic, parsley, butter and mushrooms. Continue to sauté for a further 2 minutes until all the ingredients are soft.

3 Pour in the double cream and bring to the boil, then reduce the heat and allow the sauce to simmer for 3–4 minutes to thicken slightly.

4 Serve warm with freshly boiled pasta (see page 68).

BEST FOR BABY Do experiment with other mushrooms for a little variation: try chestnut, oyster, portobella or the large, flat, open mushrooms. All are nutritionally beneficial and each has an incredible unique flavour.

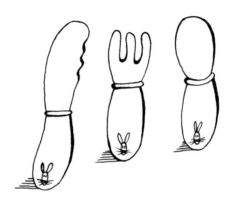

Baby pork burgers with apple

Home-made burgers are so easy – and delicious – to make. I first did these burgers on a TV programme called 'Dinner Doctors' and everyone in the family involved loved them. Best of all, the 4-year-old learned how to make them successfully for when I wasn't there!

SUITABLE FOR FREEZING

MAKES 12 SMALL BURGERS

100 g/4 oz lean minced (ground) pork

1 shallot or ½ onion, finely chopped

10 ml/2 tsp dried parsley

15 ml/1 tbsp fresh wholemeal breadcrumbs

10 ml/2 tsp tomato purée (paste)

½ eating (dessert) apple, coarsely grated, including the peel

1 egg, beaten

Unrefined sunflower oil, for cooking

1 Put the minced pork, chopped shallot or onion and parsley into a bowl.

2 Mix well and then add the breadcrumbs and tomato purée.

3 Squeeze out any excess juice from the grated apple, and add the fruit to the mixture and stir well.

4 Add the beaten egg to bind everything together. Using your hands, form the mixture into 12 small balls and flatten into little burgers.

5 Heat a little oil in a non-stick frying pan (skillet). Add the burgers and cook for 2–3 minutes on each side.

6 When the burgers are thoroughly cooked, remove from the heat to cool down slightly, then serve.

Serving suggestions Mashed potatoes and my Tomato Sauce with Garden Herbs (see page 67) would go beautifully with these.

Hints and variations Once cooked, these burgers will keep very well in the freezer for 1–3 months. You can make them with minced chicken or beef, if you prefer. For best results, use the coarsest side of the grater for the apple, and chop the onion in a food processor.

BEST FOR BABY Some commercially produced meats contain antibiotics that can be passed to your baby either directly or even through breast milk. For this reason, I would recommend that you buy 'farm-fresh' or organically produced meats for the whole family.

Home-made falafels

Falafels are simply delicious. Don't be afraid to start offering your baby small tastes of the more exotic spices such as turmeric and cumin. They provide a gentle introduction to the flavours of Eastern cooking and because neither of them is a 'hot' spice, they won't upset your baby's taste buds, or his stomach.

SUITABLE FOR FREEZING

MAKES 16–20 SMALL FALAFELS

15 ml/1 tbsp unrefined sunflower oil

½ onion, peeled and finely chopped

2.5 ml/½ tsp ground cumin

2.5 ml/½ tsp ground turmeric

225 g/8 oz/medium can of chickpeas (garbanzos), drained

1 garlic clove, peeled and crushed

45 ml/3 tbsp tahini (sesame seed paste)

100 g/4 oz/2 cups fresh wholemeal breadcrumbs

Sea salt and freshly ground black pepper

1 egg, beaten

1 Preheat the oven 190°C/375°F/gas 5/fan oven 170°C.

2 Heat the oil in a medium-large saucepan. Add the onion and spices. Sauté for 1–2 minutes, then add the drained chickpeas.

3 Cook for 1 minute, then stir in the garlic and tahini.

4 Remove from the heat and add the breadcrumbs. Mash everything together using a potato masher and season very lightly to taste.

5 Leave to cool slightly, then add the beaten egg to bind everything together. Using your hands, mould the mixture into little balls or patties.

6 Place on a greased and lined baking (cookie) tray and bake in the oven for about 20 minutes until golden brown.

7 Serve warm, or cool, then freeze.

Serving suggestions Falafels are great served with a home-made tomato sauce – you could use the one on page 67 – or some vegetables, or you could slice them and use to fill sandwiches with a little mango chutney and crisp salad for Mum and Dad to enjoy.

Hints and variations Tahini is widely available in supermarkets and health food shops.

BEST FOR BABY Sesame seeds are a rich source of calcium and a great support food during pregnancy and whilst breast-feeding. The oil from sesame seeds contains vitamin E and is a natural sunscreen.

★ encourage children to help choose fresh foods

cakes and treats are a good way to introduce fruit into any diet

Corn bread

Corn bread is not only fun to make, but it also has a wonderful texture to liven the senses of a young baby. Once you have mastered the basic recipe, you can start to add other ingredients that you would like your baby to try, such as fresh herbs or different types of cheese and vegetables.

SUITABLE FOR FREEZING

MAKES 1 LARGE LOAF

275 g/10 oz/2½ cups self-raising (self-rising) flour

225 g/8 oz/2 cups cornmeal

50 g/2 oz/¼ cup unrefined caster (superfine) sugar

15 ml/1 tbsp baking powder

4 large eggs, beaten

600 ml/1 pt/2½ cups full-fat milk

100 g/4 oz/½ cup butter, melted

1 Preheat the oven to 200°C/400°F/gas 6/fan oven 180°C.

2 In a large bowl, mix all the dry ingredients together.

3 Add the beaten eggs, milk and melted butter and beat well for a couple of minutes until smooth.

4 Tip the bread mix into a greased shallow 30 x 23 cm/12 x 9 in baking tin (pan).

5 Bake in the oven for 30–35 minutes or until golden brown and firm to the touch.

6 Remove from the oven, allow to cool a little, then cut into slices and serve warm.

Serving suggestions This corn bread is always best served warm, but it does make a delicious packed-lunch addition. Try it spread with my Salmon and Fresh Mint Pâté (see page 48).

Hints and variations Cornmeal is available in supermarkets and health food shops. It may be labelled 'polenta' or 'maizemeal'.

For more texture and flavour, try adding grated cheese, cooked broccoli, peas, carrots, chopped fresh herbs, etc. Simply stir them in at Step 3.

BEST FOR BABY Cornmeal is a useful source of several minerals and vitamins. These include manganese, needed for healthy bone and cartilage formation, which is particularly important as your child's bones harden.

Oatmeal cookies

Teething usually starts at around 6–7 months, although it may be much later. These oatmeal biscuits make perfect snacks to give your baby when he starts looking for something to chew on. They have a really interesting texture for the baby and of course are extremely nutritious.

SUITABLE FOR FREEZING

MAKES 20 SMALL COOKIES

50 g/2 oz/½ cup plain (all-purpose) flour

175 g/6 oz/1½ cups oatmeal

50 g/2 oz/½ cup porridge oats

100 g/4 oz/½ cup butter

1 egg yolk

1 Preheat the oven to 180°C/350°F/gas 4/fan oven 160°C.

2 Mix all of the dry ingredients together, and then, using your fingertips, rub in the butter until the mixture resembles fine breadcrumbs.

3 Add the egg yolk and mix to a firm dough, then turn out on to a board and knead lightly.

4 Roll out quite thinly and then, using a cutter, cut into your desired shapes.

5 Place on a greased and lined baking (cookie) tray and bake in the oven for about 15 minutes or until golden brown.

6 Cool on a wire rack.

BEST FOR BABY Oats in any form are believed to help prevent infection and guard against contagious diseases, particularly in children.

GETTING CHEWY: 9-12 MONTHS

Semolina pudding with mixed berries

Semolina is, in my opinion, a totally underrated grain and makes a wonderful dessert for babies, toddlers and adults. This is a classic semolina pudding, which goes very well with most fruit. I've used mixed frozen berries in this recipe as they are so economical and readily available.

SUITABLE FOR FREEZING

MAKES 6 BABY PORTIONS

25 g/1 oz/2 tbsp butter

10 ml/2 tsp natural vanilla essence (extract)

100 g/4 oz/1/2 cup unrefined caster (superfine) sugar

1 litre/1³/₄ pts/4¹/₄ cups full-fat milk

100 g/4 oz/²/₃ cup semolina (cream of wheat)

300 ml/¹/₂ pt/1¹/₄ cups double (heavy) cream

100 g/4 oz thawed frozen mixed berries

1 Place the butter, vanilla, sugar and milk in a saucepan and bring to the boil.

2 Pour in the semolina, whisking while you add it. Turn down the heat and cook, stirring continuously, until the mixture thickens.

3 Pour in the double cream and leave to simmer for a few minutes.

4 Meanwhile, drain any excess juice from the berries and arrange in a layer in a serving dish.

5 Pour the thick semolina cream over the berries.

6 Serve warm or allow the dessert to cool before serving.

Serving suggestions You can drizzle honey over once your child is over one year of age.

Hints and variations Try making this with other fruits – pear, apple, fresh strawberries and even sliced banana all work well.

BEST FOR BABY Semolina is produced by sifting and separating wheat grains that have had their outer coating removed. We know it best as a dessert but it may also be mixed with water and flour, to make couscous. In either form it is a useful source of both protein and minerals.

Basic rice pudding

The lovely creamy texture is a great favourite with babies and here I've added a little vanilla essence to liven it up. On page 78, you will find a more exotic version to try. Both freeze well, so it is a good idea to make a large batch and then freeze it in convenient quantities.

SUITABLE FOR FREEZING

MAKES 12 BABY PORTIONS

75 g/3 oz/¹/₃ cup round-grain (pudding) rice

50 g/2 oz/¹/₄ cup unrefined caster (superfine) sugar

900 ml/1¹/₂ pts/3³/₄ cups full-fat milk

2.5 ml/¹/₂ tsp natural vanilla essence (extract)

25 g/1 oz/2 tbsp butter

1 Preheat the oven to 160°C/350°F/gas 4/fan oven 140°C.

2 Place the rice, sugar, milk and vanilla in a shallow baking dish. Dot over the butter and then place in the oven for about 1¹/₂–1³/₄ hours.

3 Allow to cool a little before serving.

Serving suggestions This is delicious served warm or cold with some Simple Apple Pureé (see page 40).

Hints and variations Because the cooking time is so long, I would recommend that you make a double quantity and then freeze it. Once cooked, allow the pudding to cool completely, then divide into individual baby portions or family-sized quantities.

Dairy-free rice pudding

A large number of children seem to suffer from an intolerance to cows' milk (see Allergies and intolerances, page 23) so I have included this dairy-free version of rice pudding, which is delicious as well as being very nutritious. Always check with your doctor before cutting milk out of your child's diet.

SUITABLE FOR FREEZING

MAKES 12 BABY PORTIONS

75 g/3 oz/⅓ cup round-grain (pudding) rice

50 g/2 oz/¼ cup unrefined caster (superfine) sugar

900 ml/1½ pts/3¾ cups soya milk

25 g/1 oz raisins

25 g/½ oz/1 tbsp butter

1 Preheat the oven to 160°C/325°F/gas 3/fan oven 145°C.

2 Place the rice, sugar, milk and raisins in a shallow baking dish. Dot over the butter and then place in the oven for about 1½–1¾ hours.

3 Allow to cool a little before serving.

Serving suggestions Like ordinary rice pudding, this is delicious with stewed or puréed fruit of any kind.

Mango and coconut rice pudding

As I said earlier, rice pudding really doesn't have to be dull! This recipe gives a tropical twist to the traditional version, using coconut milk and mango. It is ideal for young children as it uses far less sugar than the canned varieties, and it should go down well with the whole family.

SUITABLE FOR FREEZING

MAKES 8–10 BABY PORTIONS

75 g/3 oz/⅓ cup round-grain (pudding) rice

10 ml/2 tsp natural vanilla extract (essence)

50 g/2 oz/½ cup desiccated (shredded) coconut

40 g/1½ oz/scant ¼ cup unrefined caster (superfine) sugar

1 whole mango, peeled, stoned (pitted) and diced

400 ml/14 fl oz/1¾ cups coconut milk

400 ml/14 fl oz/1¾ cups full-fat milk

25 g/1 oz/2 tbsp butter

1 Preheat the oven to 160°C/325°F/gas 3/fan oven 145°C.

2 In a shallow baking dish place the rice, vanilla, coconut, sugar, diced mango and both the milks. Dot the top with tiny pieces of butter.

3 Place the dish in the oven and bake for about 1½–1¾ hours, stirring occasionally, until the rice is tender and the top is crisp and golden.

4 Remove from the oven and leave to cool a little before serving.

5 If freezing, leave to cool completely, then divide into individual portions or smaller quantities.

Serving suggestions Serve this rice pudding on its own for young babies or warm with vanilla ice cream for a family dessert.

BEST FOR BABY Coconut milk is highly nutritious, with a similar chemical composition to mothers' milk. Its digestive properties and high amino acid content make it wonderful for mums during pregnancy as well as for baby afterwards.

tasty treats for toddlers:

food on the move

Whatever you do to avoid it, at some point your toddler is going to recognise what treats, snacks and sweets are. Don't try to prevent this – it makes perfect sense to allow him to enjoy them, as long as you educate him at the same time as to when to eat them. The trick is to make him understand that each one is delicious little extra treat, not a substitute for a meal.

There are plenty of ready-made snacks and sweets on sale at the supermarket. But for me, of course, the best food is home-made food and the tasty recipes in this chapter reflect this. They have all been designed to use the least amount of sugar and to make full use of ingredients as close to their natural state as possible whilst not compromising on taste, texture and colour.

This is also your chance to introduce your toddler to cooking – yes, really! Your child will start to learn simple techniques, gain confidence about preparing food and, of course, build up an appetite to eat what he has created, which is a wonderful experience. True, it's a messy business at first, but a few sheets of newspaper on the floor will help to make the clean-up operation simpler. And it will be worth it when you see the pride on your toddler's face as the whole family tucks into the treats he has made!

Foods you can introduce at three years

Once your child is three, whole grains and nuts (see Allergies and intolerances, page 23) can be introduced to his diet but remember that young children should never be given nuts or other similar-sized hard foods unsupervised just in case they become stuck in their throat. If that does happen, lay them swiftly across your lap and hit them firmly on their back so that the food is expelled.

Golden crispy potatoes

These potatoes provide a perfect alternative to those shop-bought oven chips and funny-faced potato shapes that are so popular with your toddler and his friends! Don't add salt before cooking as this prevents them the potatoes from crisping and try to go easy on the ketchup – it contains masses of sugar.

NOT SUITABLE FOR FREEZING

MAKES 4–6 BABY PORTIONS

1 kg/2¼ lb floury potatoes

60 ml/4 tbsp olive oil

4 garlic cloves, peeled and crushed

10 ml/2 tsp dried thyme

Sea salt and freshly ground black pepper

1 Preheat the oven to 200°C/400°F/gas 6/fan oven 180°C.

2 Peel and cut the potatoes into 2 cm/¾ in dice. Toss in a bowl with the oil, garlic and thyme.

3 Spread the potatoes out in a large, shallow roasting tin (pan) and roast for 30–35 minutes until nicely golden brown.

4 Turn them over and return to the oven for 10–15 minutes until golden and very crisp. Sprinkle over sea salt and pepper – be sparing when seasoning your baby's portion.

5 Allow to cool a little, then serve.

Serving suggestions As well as the perfect accompaniment for your baby's main course, these are also delicious dipped into my Button Mushroom and Cheddar Cheese Dip (see page 65) or Two-cheese Fondue with Cider (see page 120).

BEST FOR THE FAMILY Garlic may help to bring down fever and is a highly effective decongestant too.

Express pizzas

Kids generally love pizzas, particularly if they can choose their own toppings. Sadly modern-day life leaves very little time to make the traditional fermented yeast pizza dough but this incredible quick pizza base, which uses a natural chemical reaction of live yoghurt and self-raising flour, is almost as good.

SUITABLE FOR FREEZING WHEN COOKED

MAKES 8 CHILD'S PORTIONS OR 4 SMALL PIZZAS

FOR THE PIZZA DOUGH

125 g/4½ oz/good 1 cup self-raising (self-rising) wholemeal flour

125 g/4½ oz/good 1 cup self-raising white flour

2.5 ml/½ tsp dried mixed herbs

200 ml/7 fl oz/scant 1 cup full-fat plain set live yoghurt

A tiny pinch of sea salt

FOR THE TOPPING

100 ml/3½ fl oz/scant ½ cup tomato purée (paste)

Additional toppings to suit, e.g. baby sweetcorn (corn), sliced mushrooms, fresh herbs, diced salami, etc.

200 g/7 oz/scant 1 cup grated full-fat Cheddar or Red Leicester cheese

1 Preheat the oven to 200°C/400°F/gas 6/fan oven 180°C.

2 Mix the flours, herbs, yoghurt and salt together to form a soft but not sticky dough. If the dough is too wet, then add more flour. If it's too dry, add more yoghurt.

3 Roll the dough out on the lightly floured surface to make the desired pizza shape you require. Place on a greased baking (cookie) tray.

4 Spread over the tomato purée and sprinkle generously with grated cheese, then add any extra toppings of your choice.

5 Place in the oven to cook for about 20–25 minutes or until crisp and golden brown.

BEST FOR THE FAMILY Wholemeal flour is packed full of fibre and other important nutrients but its dense texture may be less attractive to young children than white. Mixing half wholemeal with half white flour is a great way of gently encouraging them to enjoy the taste.

Traditional crisp pizza base

This is the way that authentic pizzas are traditionally made. You will need to plan ahead in order to allow for the fermentation time of the yeast but I think it's well worth the effort. The results are crisp, light and delicious. You can use the same method of topping as for the pizza on page 82.

About 100 ml/3½ fl oz/scant ½ cup hand-hot water

2.5 ml/½ tsp unrefined caster (superfine) sugar

7.5 ml/1½ tsp dried yeast

225 g/8 oz/2 cups plain (all-purpose) flour

5 ml/1 tsp sea salt

1 egg, beaten

15 ml/1 tbsp extra-virgin olive oil

1 Pour the water into a basin and whisk in the sugar, followed by the yeast. Leave to one side for about 10–15 minutes until it has a nice frothy head on it.

2 Meanwhile, sift the flour and salt together in a mixing bowl. Pour in the frothy yeast mixture and the beaten egg and mix well. You should end up with a soft pliable dough that leaves the bowl clean.

3 Transfer the dough to a working surface and knead for 10 minutes until silky smooth and elastic.

4 Rub the surface of the dough with oil, then place in a bowl, cover tightly with clingfilm (plastic wrap) or a damp tea towel (dish cloth). Put in a warmish place to rise for about an hour or until it has doubled in size.

5 Meanwhile, preheat the oven to 200°C/400°F/gas 6/fan oven 180°C.

6 Knock back (punch down) the dough to remove the air and roll out to make your pizza base.

7 Add the toppings of your choice (see page 82), then cook in the preheated oven for about 20–25 minutes or until crisp and golden brown.

Mini fish balls

Fish fingers are a great children's favourite, so why not try these crisp salmon fish balls for a change? They are made using canned salmon, which is not only incredibly nutritious, but also a convenient storecupboard item. This recipe is gluten- and wheat-free.

SUITABLE FOR FREEZING ONCE COOKED

MAKES ABOUT 12–16 SMALL BALLS

225 g/8 oz waxy potatoes, peeled and cut into dice

25 g/1 oz canned red salmon, drained

10 ml/2 tsp paprika

10 ml/2 tsp dried parsley

10 ml/2 tsp dried chives

Sea salt and freshly ground black pepper

1 large egg, beaten

30–45 ml/2–3 tbsp polenta (cornmeal)

15 ml/1 tbsp unrefined sunflower oil

25 g/1 oz/2 tbsp butter

1 Place the potato pieces in a pan of water and bring to the boil. Cook for 12–14 minutes or until soft. Drain and then return to the same pan and set over a low heat to dry a little.

2 Add the salmon, paprika, herbs and season very lightly, then mash the ingredients over the heat for about 1 minute.

3 Add the beaten egg and mix quickly. (Adding the egg too early may cause it to scramble slightly.)

4 Add 15 ml/1 tbsp of the polenta and stir the potato and fish mixture until it forms a firm dough-like consistency.

5 Spread the mixture out on a baking (cookie) tray to cool quickly. Once cool enough to handle, using your hands, shape the mixture into balls about the size of a golf ball and dust with the remaining polenta.

6 Heat the oil in a large frying pan (skillet). Add the fish balls, followed by the butter. Cook, moving the fish balls around all the time so that they become crisp all over.

7 Serve warm.

Serving suggestions These go perfectly with my Lentil and Carrot Dhal (see page 66).

Hints and variations These fish balls can be prepared in advance and then reheated in a hot oven at 180°C/350°F/gas 6/fan oven 160°C for about 10 minutes. Polenta is widely available at health food shops and food stores.

BEST FOR THE FAMILY Salmon is a rich source of omega 3, an essential fatty acid – 'essential' because the body cannot make it and must therefore find it from food sources. Our brains need omega 3 essential fats in order to function properly. This is perhaps why fish is known as a 'brain food'.

Savoury cheese cakes

These little savoury Welsh cakes are a wonderful family standby – I would recommend that you always keep a stock of them in your freezer. They not only make fabulous toddler snack items but are also delicious for tired and often hungry older children when they come in from school.

SUITABLE FOR FREEZING

MAKES 16–18 SMALL CAKES

100 g/4 oz/1 cup self-raising (self-rising) white flour

125 g/4½ oz/good 1 cup self-raising wholemeal flour

100 g/4 oz/½ cup butter

100 g/4 oz/½ cup grated full-fat Cheddar or Red Leicester cheese

25 g/1 oz/¼ cup chopped mixed nuts (optional)

A tiny pinch of cayenne

1 large egg, beaten

15 ml/1 tbsp unrefined sunflower oil, for cooking

1 Mix the flours together, add the butter and, using your fingertips, rub in to the consistency of breadcrumbs.

2 Add the cheese, nuts (if using), cayenne and egg, then stir until the mixture forms a dough. Alternatively, use a food processor to speed things up – but not if children are making these unsupervised.

3 Grease a flat-based griddle or large non-stick frying pan (skillet) with a little sunflower oil and place on a low heat.

4 On a floured surface, roll out the dough to a thickness of 1 cm/½ in. Stamp out rounds using a suitable cutter and re-roll any trimmings.

5 Place the cakes gently on the griddle or frying pan and cook for 3–4 minutes on each side until golden brown.

6 Leave to cool, preferably on a wire rack, before serving.

Serving suggestions These Welsh cakes are delicious served with a little cream cheese or pâté.

Hints and variations To reheat from frozen, place one in the microwave and cook on High (100 per cent power) for 20–30 seconds.

BEST FOR YOUR BABY Red-hot cayenne was brought from India in the mid-sixteenth century and Westerners have used it ever since for its warming properties. Particularly useful in the winter months, it is great for sniffles, chills and improving circulation (beware, though, only the tiniest pinch is needed).

TASTY TREATS FOR TODDLERS: FOOD ON THE MOVE

Cheesy twigs

Fun to make, these savoury snacks are a perfect reward for good behaviour. Children love them – and so do mums and dads! The mixture is very simple to make so even your youngest toddler can help you stir it up, and children will enjoy rolling them into all sort of shapes and sizes.

SUITABLE FOR FREEZING

MAKES 8–10 PORTIONS

100 g/4 oz/1 cup plain
(all-purpose) flour

100 g/4 oz/1 cup self-raising
(self-rising) wholemeal flour

5 ml/1 tsp paprika

100 g/4 oz/¹⁄₂ cup ricotta cheese

100 g/4 oz/¹⁄₂ cup full-fat cream cheese

200 g/7 oz/scant 1 cup butter, softened

2 eggs, beaten

1 Preheat the oven to 220°C/425°F/gas 7/fan oven 200°C.

2 In a large mixing bowl, mix the flours and paprika together.

3 Add the two cheeses and softened butter and gently combine until the mixture looks like breadcrumbs.

4 Reserve a little of the beaten egg and add the remainder to the bowl. Mix everything together until the ingredients form a ball. Wrap and chill in the freezer for 20 minutes. (This will make it much easier to roll out the dough.)

5 Roll out the dough on a floured surface as thinly as possible and then brush with the reserved beaten egg.

6 Cut into long strips for twigs, or make any other shapes you wish. Lay the shapes on a greased baking (cookie) tray.

7 Bake for 10–12 minutes or until golden brown.

8 Remove from the oven and allow to cool slightly before serving.

Hints and variations Try adding some aromatic seeds such as sesame, fennel or even coriander (cilantro). This will help your children to develop tastes for different, but subtle natural flavourings.

BEST FOR THE FAMILY Coriander seeds are another very effective cure for wind. Just add 5 ml/1 tsp of crushed seeds to a glass of warm water. Try for yourself – it really works.

Giant raisin and walnut cookies

There is simply no smell better than that of home-made cookies. This recipe is a one-bowl wonder and many of the children I have given cookery demonstrations to have enjoyed them. For some reason, it seems that the giant size makes them taste even better!

SUITABLE FOR FREEZING

MAKES 8–10 GIANT COOKIES

100 g/4 oz/¹/₂ cup non-hydrogenated margarine

100 g/4 oz/¹/₂ cup unrefined soft light brown sugar

A few drops of natural vanilla essence (extract)

175 g/6 oz/1¹/₂ cups self-raising (self-rising) flour

50 g/2 oz/¹/₂ cup walnut pieces, crushed

100 g/4 oz/²/₃ cup raisins

1 large egg, beaten

2.5 ml/¹/₂ tsp bicarbonate of soda (baking soda)

A pinch of ground cinnamon

1 Preheat the oven to 190°C/375°F/gas 5/fan oven 170°C.

2 Put the margarine, sugar and vanilla into a mixing bowl. Beat well for about 3–4 minutes until the mixture is creamy and pale-coloured. (It is easier if you use a food processor, but don't let your child use it unsupervised.)

3 Add the walnuts to the bowl with the raisins, egg, bicarbonate of soda and cinnamon and mix together well.

4 Grease and line two baking (cookie) trays with baking parchment and then divide the cookie dough into 8–10 portions.

5 Mould the dough into balls and then gently press each one down to flatten slightly.

6 Bake in the oven for 15–17 minutes or until golden and firm to the touch. Allow the cookies to cool before transferring to an airtight container.

BEST FOR THE FAMILY Walnuts are a rich source of the mineral zinc. Zinc is required for over 200 enzyme activities in the body and is vital for growth and sexual development. It is also key to a healthy immune system and assists in our ability to taste foods.

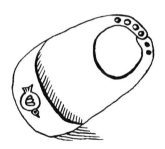

Mini apple and oat drop scones

Easy and fun to make, these drop scones are like thick but light pancakes. They are so popular, you may have trouble cooling them before the children start to eat them! Your toddler will enjoy helping you to make the mixture, though you should make sure you keep them well away from the hot frying pan.

SUITABLE FOR FREEZING

MAKES 24 SMALL OR 12 MEDIUM-SIZED SCONES

50 g/2 oz/¼ cup butter, softened

225 g/1 oz/2 tbsp self-raising (self-rising) flour

100 g/4 oz/1 cup rolled oats

A pinch of ground cinnamon

25 g/1 oz/2 tbsp unrefined caster (superfine) sugar

1 large egg, beaten

2 unpeeled eating (dessert) apples, washed and coarsely grated

100 ml/4 fl oz/scant ½ cup full-fat plain Greek yoghurt

A little unrefined sunflower oil

1 Mix the butter into the flour, and then stir in the oats, cinnamon and sugar. Gradually add the beaten egg and stir in the grated apples with their juice.

2 Heat a heavy frying pan (skillet) on a medium to high heat and lightly grease with sunflower oil.

3 Drop tablespoons of the mixture into the pan and cook for about 1 minute on each side.

4 Remove the scones (biscuits) from the pan and place on kitchen roll (paper towels) to absorb any grease.

Serving suggestions Sift together equal quantities of cinnamon and icing (confectioners') sugar and sprinkle over the scones before serving. Spread with butter and eat as snacks. They also make a good addition to lunch boxes.

Hints and variations To freeze the pancakes, make them without the apple and yoghurt, then, once completely cold, place between layers of baking parchment, then wrap and seal. When ready to eat, thaw in the microwave on High (100 per cent power) for 30 seconds.

BEST FOR THE FAMILY Oats and apples are two good sources of soluble fibre, which helps the function of the digestive tract and maintains balanced blood sugar levels.

Foolproof chocolate brownies

In my time as a chef, I have collected literally dozens of recipes for chocolate brownies. This one is my favourite. It is absolutely fail-safe and so delicious that you may need to double the quantities! In fact, the brownies are so moist and delicate I often serve them as a dinner party dessert.

SUITABLE FOR FREEZING

MAKES ABOUT 12–14 MEDIUM SLICES

225 g/8 oz/1 cup unsalted (sweet) butter

125 g/4½ oz plain (semi-sweet) chocolate, broken up

3 eggs

275 g/10 oz/1¼ cups unrefined caster (superfine) sugar

175 g/6 oz/1½ cups plain (all-purpose) flour

175 g/6 oz/1½ cups self-raising (self-rising) flour

25 g/1 oz/2 tbsp organic cocoa (unsweetened chocolate) powder

50 g/2 oz/½ cup walnut pieces

125 g/4½ oz/good 1 cup white chocolate drops

1 Preheat the oven to 180°C/350°F/gas 4/fan oven 160°C.

2 Place the butter and plain chocolate into a bowl and then sit the bowl on top of a pan of boiling water (the water should not touch the bowl). Heat, stirring the chocolate and butter together occasionally, until they have both melted.

3 Beat the eggs and sugar together until they become light and thick. Gently fold this mixture into the melted chocolate and butter.

4 Mix the two flours, cocoa powder, walnuts and white chocolate together, then stir into the melted chocolate mixture.

5 Lightly grease a deep baking tin (pan) and, if the tray is not non-stick, line with baking parchment. Pour the mixture into the tin and place in the oven. Cook for 30 minutes or until the surface is firm to the touch.

6 Allow to cool, then slice and serve.

Serving suggestions Serve with some crème fraîche or vanilla ice cream as they may be little rich served on their own.

BEST FOR THE FAMILY Look out for the 'Fair trade' mark when you buy chocolate. It is an independent guarantee that a fair price has been set for the cocoa beans and therefore offers the Third World farmers a reasonable return on their yields. It also ensures child labour has been prohibited in production, and plantation workers have decent wages, safety standards and democratic rights.

Apricot and chocolate chip muffins

These muffins are very easy to make! They contain lots of apple to help keep them moist and naturally sweet and, if you are looking for something to reward good behaviour, they make a delicious alternative to sweets. However, your children will still need to brush their teeth after eating them.

MAKES 10–12 MUFFINS

90 g/3½ oz/scant ½ cup butter, melted

25 g/1 oz/2 tbsp dried unsulphured apricots

175 g/6 oz coarsely grated unpeeled eating (dessert) apple, any juice reserved

250 g/9 oz/2¼ cups unbleached white self-raising (self-rising) flour

50 g/2 oz/¼ cup unrefined caster (superfine) sugar

50 g/2 oz/½ cup milk (sweet) chocolate buttons or chips

1 egg, beaten

100 ml/3½ fl oz/scant 1 cup full-fat or semi-skimmed milk

1 Preheat the oven to 190°C/375°F/gas 5/fan oven 170°C.

2 Brush a muffin tray with a little of the melted butter.

3 Snip the apricots into thin strips with a pair of scissors and place in a bowl with the grated apple and the juice.

4 Put the flour, sugar, chocolate, egg and remaining melted butter into a large mixing bowl (use a food processor if you prefer). Start to mix and immediately pour in the milk and add the fruit mixture.

5 Beat thoroughly until you have a smooth batter. Spoon the batter into the muffin tins and bake in the oven for 20–22 minutes or until they turn golden brown and are firm to the touch.

6 Remove from the oven and allow to cool before storing in an airtight container – if they last that long!

Hints and variations Don't worry if the apple starts to go dark once it is grated. This will actually help the colour of the muffins.

BEST FOR THE FAMILY Apples are rich in phosphorus, which is believed to help with bone and tooth structure.

Carrot and banana cake

A well-made, moist carrot cake with cream cheese icing is pure heaven. There are lots of recipes, but since I developed this one, which contains banana too, I use no other. It is easy to make, full of good things, almost foolproof, always moist and freezes beautifully.

SUITABLE FOR FREEZING

MAKES 12–14 SLICES

FOR THE CAKE
225 g/8 oz/2 cups self-raising (self-rising) flour

10 ml/2 tsp baking powder

150 g/5 oz/²⁄₃ cup unrefined muscovado sugar

100 g/4 oz/1 cup grated carrot

2 ripe bananas, peeled and mashed

2 eggs

150 ml/¹⁄₄ pt/²⁄₃ cup unrefined sunflower oil

10 ml/2 tsp ground cinnamon

50 g/2 oz/¹⁄₂ cup walnut pieces, chopped or crushed

FOR THE ICING (FROSTING)
75 g/3 oz/¹⁄₃ cup butter, softened

175 g/6 oz/1 cup icing (confectioners') sugar, sifted

A few drops of natural vanilla essence (extract)

225 g/8 oz/1 cup full-fat cream cheese

1 Preheat the oven to 180°C/350°F/gas 4/fan oven 160°C. Grease a 23 cm/9 in flan tin (pie pan) or 900 g/2 lb loaf tin.

2 Place all of the cake ingredients except the walnuts in a bowl.

3 Beat well until smooth, then fold in the nuts.

4 Pour the mixture into the prepared tin, then bake in the oven for about 30–35 minutes or until firm to the touch.

5 Meanwhile, make the icing. Place the butter and icing sugar in a mixing bowl and beat until pale and fluffy. Add the vanilla and cream cheese and continue to mix until smooth.

6 Remove the cake from the oven and cool completely on a wire rack. Cover it with the cream cheese icing, then slice and serve.

BEST FOR THE FAMILY Carrots contain lots of beta-carotene, which is thought to help to increase the body's protection against some cancers. Try introducing carrot juice to your young one's diet: it's a real 'super-juice', rich in vitamins and minerals. Younger palates may prefer it mixed with orange juice.

Date and apple sandwich slices

These fruit sandwiches are such fun to make, you can get your toddler and their friends involved in the preparation with adult supervision. I've used apple and dates in this recipe, but you could use pear, apricots or even peaches. The nuts and dates are best chopped in a food processor.

SUITABLE FOR FREEZING

MAKES ABOUT 10–12 MEDIUM SLICES

FOR THE FILLING

120 ml/4 fl oz/½ cup water

30 ml/2 tbsp clear honey

225 g/8 oz/1⅓ cups stoned (pitted) dates, finely chopped

Juice of ½ lemon

125 g/4½ oz peeled and coarsely grated apple (prepared weight)

50 g/2 oz/½ cup brazil nuts, finely chopped

FOR THE BASE

115 g/4½ oz/good ⅔ cup semolina (cream of wheat)

115 g/4½ oz/good 1 cup self-raising (self-rising) flour

115 g/4½ oz/good ½ cup non-hydrogenated margarine

25 g/1 oz/2 tbsp unrefined soft brown sugar

50 g/2 oz/½ cup brazil nuts, finely chopped

1 Preheat the oven to 190°C/375°F/gas 5/fan oven 170°C.

2 To make the filling, mix the water and honey together in a saucepan and add the chopped dates. Simmer for for 5–6 minutes until the ingredients soften into a purée.

3 Stir in the lemon juice, apple and nuts and leave the mixture to cool slightly.

4 Meanwhile, make the base. Mix the semolina with the flour. Add the margarine and rub together with your fingertips to the consistency of breadcrumbs. Stir in the sugar and chopped nuts.

5 Spread half of this mix over the base of a greased 23 cm/9 in flan tin (pie pan). Pour the filling over this and then cover with the remaining base mixture to form a 'sandwich'.

6 Bake in the oven for 35–40 minutes until golden and firm to the touch. It is a good idea to cover the top with a sheet of foil after 10–15 minutes to stop it over-browning.

7 Remove from the oven and leave in the tin to cool. Slice, then serve warm.

Serving suggestions Serve as a dessert with thick custard.

Hints and variations When completely cold, the slices can be stored in an airtight container for 3–4 days. They can also be frozen. To reheat, place in a moderate oven for 10 minutes or in the microwave on High (100 per cent power) for 1–2 minutes.

BEST FOR THE FAMILY Nuts are real energy-providers, packed full of essential fats and minerals that young children need. However, when introducing them into your toddler's diet, watch carefully for any sign of skin irritation or discomfort. If you suspect he has a sensitivity to nuts, consult your doctor without delay.

Pineapple and banana meringue pots

This is an unusual but very useful recipe that contains mostly storecupboard ingredients. It is extremely economical and makes a good starter recipe for budding young chefs. However, do remember that you need to be around to supervise when they are using hot pans.

SUITABLE FOR FREEZING

MAKES 4 SMALL POTS

225 g/8 oz/small can of pineapple pieces in natural juice

45 ml/3 tbsp cornflour (cornstarch)

2 large eggs, separated

425 ml/14½ fl oz/good 1¾ cups full-fat or semi-skimmed milk

5 ml/1 tsp natural vanilla essence (extract)

50 g/2 oz/¼ cup unrefined caster (superfine) sugar

2 bananas

1 Preheat the oven to 190°C/375°F/gas 5/fan oven 170°C.

2 Drain the pineapple juice into a medium-sized pan. Blend in the cornflour, then stir in the egg yolks, milk and vanilla essence.

3 Heat, stirring all the time with a small whisk or wooden spoon, until the mixture boils and thickens.

4 Reduce the heat and cook gently for 1 minute, stirring all the time.

5 Remove the pan from the heat and stir in half the sugar and all the pineapple.

6 Slice the bananas, add to the mixture and stir everything together gently. Taste and add a little more sugar if the sauce is not sweet enough.

7 Spoon the mix into four individual baking dishes and set on a baking (cookie) tray. Bake in the oven for 5 minutes.

8 Whisk the egg whites with an electric hand beater until they hold their shape. Tip in the remaining sugar and whisk until the meringue is glossy. Pile on to the hot desserts, then return to the oven and bake for 5 minutes until golden.

9 Serve warm.

BEST FOR THE FAMILY It is widely known that bananas contain high levels of potassium, vital for muscle and nerve function. Bananas are also great for stomach upsets. The riper they are, the better – just blend them with a little live yoghurt for a delicious soothing snack.

Bread and butter pudding with marmalade

Bread and butter pudding is always a family favourite and it's a really economical dessert, ideal to serve the family during the cold, dark autumn and winter months. Here I've dressed it up with the addition of some chunky home-made marmalade, which gives it colour and a wonderful tangy taste.

SUITABLE FOR FREEZING

MAKES 6–8 SMALL PORTIONS

2 whole eggs

2 egg yolks

125 g/4½ oz/good ½ cup unrefined caster (superfine) sugar

350 ml/12 fl oz/1⅓ cups double (heavy) or single (light) cream

350 ml/12 fl oz/1⅓ cups full-fat or semi-skimmed milk

5 ml/1 tsp natural vanilla essence (extract)

A pinch of freshly grated nutmeg

14 slices of white bread, crusts removed

100 g/4 oz/½ cup butter, softened

100 g/4 oz/⅔ cup sultanas (golden raisins)

75 g/3 oz/¼ cup orange marmalade

1 Preheat the oven to 190°C/375°C/gas 5/fan oven 170°C. Grease a 23 cm/9 in flan tin (pie pan) or 900 g/2 lb loaf tin.

2 Beat together the eggs and egg yolks, then mix with the sugar in a large mixing bowl. Slowly add the cream, milk, vanilla and nutmeg, stirring well all the time.

3 Spread the slices of bread with the butter. Put a layer of bread into the base of the baking dish, and sprinkle over the sultanas. Top with the remainder of the slices of bread.

4 Carefully pour over the egg and cream mixture and set aside for about 10 minutes to allow the liquid to soak into the bread.

5 Bake in the oven for 20–25 minutes. I think that it is always best to slightly undercook bread and butter pudding so that the finished dish has a slightly runny sauce. A deep tray of water at the bottom of the oven will help make the pudding extra moist.

6 Heat the marmalade in the microwave or in a pan on the hob and then gently brush over the pudding before serving.

Serving suggestions Bread and butter pudding is lovely served with vanilla ice cream or custard. It is also delicious cold the next day so it makes a great lunch-box addition.

BEST FOR THE FAMILY Nutmeg is calming and soothing, helping to induce sleep when used in small quantities. For a relaxing bedtime drink for older children and adults alike, add 5 ml/1 tsp of honey to a glass of hot milk with 2.5 ml/½ tsp of grated nutmeg.

Easy baked lemon cheesecake

Introduce the concept of cheese in a cake at an early age to your young family and they will not find the idea too bizarre later in life. Cheesecakes come in two types – cooked and uncooked. This is one of the former, but it is still very simple to make, and has a wonderful tangy flavour.

SUITABLE FOR FREEZING

MAKES 6–8 ADULT PORTIONS

FOR THE BASE
50 g/2 oz/¼ cup butter

125 g/4½ oz/good 1 cup crushed digestive biscuits (Graham crackers)

25 g/1 oz/2 tbsp unrefined caster (superfine) sugar

10 ml/2 tsp grated lemon zest

FOR THE FILLING
50 g/2 oz/¼ cup butter, softened

75 g/3 oz/⅓ cup unrefined caster (superfine) sugar

3 large eggs, separated

45 ml/3 tbsp lemon juice

450 g/1 lb/2 cups full-fat cream cheese

1 Preheat the oven to 160°C/325°C/gas 3/fan oven 145°C. Grease and line a 23 cm/9 in loose-bottomed flan tin (pie pan).

2 First make the base. Melt the butter and mix with the biscuit crumbs, sugar and lemon zest. Press into the flan tin.

3 Now make the filling. Cream the butter with the sugar and gradually beat in the egg yolks, followed by the lemon juice and cream cheese.

4 Whisk the whites into soft peaks. Add a little to the butter mix and beat in, then gently fold in the remaining egg whites.

5 Spoon the mixture into the flan tin and set on a baking (cookie) tray. Bake in the oven for about 1 hour or until the cheesecake is just firm to the touch.

6 Leave to cool completely, then remove from the tin, slice and serve.

Serving suggestions It is good enough to be served on its own, but you may like to add a dollop of crème fraîche.

BEST FOR THE FAMILY Cream cheese is easily digestible and therefore an extremely suitable cheese for youngsters to eat.

Passion fruit custard slices

Children all seem to love custard so I've invented this cake specially to use lots of it. The sharpness of the passion fruit works beautifully and it's a great way of introducing new fruits to your toddler. You can make your own custard following the recipe on page 97 or buy it ready-made.

SUITABLE FOR FREEZING

MAKES 10 MEDIUM SLICES

6 passion fruit

500 ml/17 fl oz/2¼ cups thick custard

250 g/9 oz/good 1 cup butter, softened

200 g/7 oz/scant 1 cup unrefined caster (superfine) sugar

4 eggs, beaten

250 g/9 oz/2¼ cups self-raising (self-rising) flour

10 ml/2 tsp baking powder

120 ml/4 fl oz/½ cup full-fat milk

50 g/2 oz/¼ cup demerara sugar

1 Preheat the oven to 180°C/375°F/gas 4/fan oven 160°C. Grease and line two 900 g/2 lb loaf tins (pans) or one 20 cm/8 in deep, round baking tin.

2 Cut the passion fruit in half and scoop out the flesh. Mix half of the seeds with the custard in a bowl and reserve the other half.

3 Cream together the butter and sugar until pale and then slowly add the beaten eggs, mixing all of the time.

4 Add the flour and baking powder and continue to beat to a smooth batter. (This is much easier with a food processor.)

5 Now add the milk and custard and beat again before pouring into the loaf or baking tin(s).

6 Scatter over the reserved passion fruit and the demerara sugar and place in the oven to bake for about 45 minutes to 1 hour or until firm to the touch.

7 Remove from the oven and leave to cool, then slice and serve.

Hints and variations You can try using other fruits, such as raspberries or blueberries, instead of passion fruit. The idea is to introduce new fruits, so if your toddler does not like one type, then try another.

BEST FOR THE FAMILY Five portions of fruit and vegetables a day – that's what the Department of Health recommends we all have. They still count if they are eaten in conjunction with other ingredients, as in these passion fruit and custard slices, or in fresh juices.

always insist on sensible safety rules in the kitchen

children learn best when they are having fun

Thick home-made custard

Making your own thick creamy custard is a delight to the senses with its delicate aroma and beautiful yellow colour. If you prefer to buy a packet mix, look out for custard mixes that use a natural colouring from the seed of the annatto tree and curcumin, an extract of turmeric root, to colour the custard.

NOT SUITABLE FOR FREEZING

MAKES ABOUT 500 ML/17 FL OZ/2¼ CUPS

500 ml/17 fl oz/2¼ cups full-fat milk

10 ml/2 tsp natural vanilla essence (extract)

4 egg yolks

25 g/1 oz/2 tbsp unrefined caster (superfine) sugar

10 ml/2 tsp cornflour (cornstarch)

1 Put the milk and vanilla in a pan and bring to the boil.

2 Mix the egg yolks, sugar and cornflour together in a bowl. Add a little of the hot milk and whisk well.

3 Pour this mixture back into the pan of hot milk and stir gently over a low heat until the custard thickens. If the custard turns lumpy, then wait until it has thickened and then pour through a sieve (strainer), using the back of a ladle to push it through.

4 Serve warm, or cool and store in the fridge for up to 4 days.

Serving suggestions Custard is a traditional accompaniment for those nursery puddings that we all love – but it's just as good on its own or with fresh, cooked or canned fruit.

Hints and variations To turn your home-made custard into a delicious chocolate sauce, simply add 10 ml/2 tsp cocoa (unsweetened chocolate) powder to the cornflour and 50 g/2 oz plain (semi-sweet) chocolate to the milk and allow to melt before mixing in with the dry ingredients.

A pinch of cinnamon or ground ginger added to custard will give it a really interesting lively flavour.

BEST FOR THE FAMILY Goats' milk is a wholesome alternative to cows' milk and because it has a different fat structure, it is far easier to digest, making it kinder to young children's developing digestive systems.

Home-made yoghurt

Many people attribute their long life and good health to eating yoghurt and there is no doubt that yoghurt has health-giving properties. Home-made yoghurt is fun and easy to make and there is no secret to the process other than practice makes perfect. The milk powder in the recipe makes it thicker.

NOT SUITABLE FOR FREEZING

MAKES 600 ML/1 PT/2½ CUPS

600 ml/1 pt/2½ cups full-fat milk

15 ml/1 tbsp milk powder

15 ml/1 tbsp full-fat plain live yoghurt

1 Bring the milk to the boil and remove from the heat. Leave to cool, then stir in the dried milk powder. Leave to cool until slightly above blood temperature.

2 Place the yoghurt in a warm basin, add a little of the warmed milk and stir until well blended, then stir in the rest of the milk.

3 Cover and stand in a warm place, such as the airing cupboard, for up to 8 hours. The warmer the room temperature, the quicker the yoghurt will set.

4 Store in the fridge when the yoghurt is set.

Serving suggestions Yoghurt is delicious on its own, perhaps sweetened with a little honey. You can also serve it with fresh fruit or breakfast cereal, or you could offer it with cooked fruit or one of the fruit purées in the first chapter. For older children and adults, try it with crushed pistachio nuts and clear honey or maple syrup.

Hints and variations The source of the heat must stay constant during the setting time.

BEST FOR THE FAMILY Yoghurt is a wonderful source of B vitamins, including B_2 (riboflavin), vital for the release of energy from food, and B_{12}, which is needed for growth. Live yoghurt contains active bacteria, which have great therapeutic value to the stomach. Check on the label that the yoghurt is actually live – many have had all the 'friendly' bacteria killed off in the fermentation processes.

feeding the family:

a social experience

By the time your baby is a year old, you will be well past making them special meals. Treat them as an integral part of the family and they will learn to enjoy the widest varieties of foods. You can always reserve the hot curries for when they have gone to bed!

Trying to juggle all your family's nutritional needs – not to mention their individual likes and dislikes – can present quite a challenge. Financial budgets may be a bit tight too and, as they grow, children often start to become a little fussy about their food. Added to this, your household duties will increase and your temper may be tested at times. For this reason, I've made all the recipes in this chapter simple, economical and, above all, easy to follow. That said, they still offer plenty of exciting taste experiences.

Many of the recipes freeze successfully and, by making use of the freezer, you can really save yourself a great deal of time and effort. The temptation to serve ready meals will often be too great, but it's worth trying to strike a natural balance between processed meals and home-cooked food to serve to your family. If, on the whole, you and your family are following a sound, varied diet with plenty of fresh ingredients, especially fruit and vegetables, the odd ready meal or fast-food burger is not going to do anyone any harm. However, what you do want to avoid, if you are encouraging your child to grow up as healthily as possible, is a diet that contains a lot of high-fat, high-salt, high-sugar, highly processed foods.

When you do cook, even if it is in a rush, try to pour a little love into the food. Think of your family as you chop and stir. Somehow, it always makes the food taste much better and I believe it also has a healing effect on the mind and body.

Finally, do try to make sure you eat as a family at least a couple of times a week. I know it's not always easy, with today's rushed schedules, but there is nothing like sitting around a table together enjoying a home-cooked meal to bring warmth and happiness to a family home.

Chunky tomato and bacon soup

Tomato and bacon are brilliant taste partners and this soup is a perfect illustration of that. Of course, you can make a vegetarian version of this soup without using bacon if you wish, but the meat does provide a unique taste and depth of flavour that makes all the difference.

SUITABLE FOR FREEZING

MAKES 4 ADULT PORTIONS

15 ml/1 tbsp unrefined sunflower oil

8 rashers (slices) of back bacon, finely chopped

1 onion, peeled and chopped

2.5 ml/½ tsp dried thyme

8 tomatoes, roughly chopped

4 garlic cloves, peeled and crushed

15 ml/1 tbsp tomato purée (paste)

1 medium potato, peeled and cut into small dice

A pinch of sea salt

A pinch of unrefined caster (superfine) sugar

100 ml/3½ fl oz/scant 1 cup double (heavy) cream

1 litre/1¾ pts/4¼ cups vegetable stock

1 Heat the oil in a large saucepan over a high heat. Add the bacon, onion and thyme and stir over the heat for 1 minute until they begin to take on some colour.

2 Add all the remaining ingredients except the cream and vegetable stock. Continue to sauté for further 3–4 minutes.

3 Pour in the cream and stock and stir well. Bring to the boil, then reduce the heat and leave to simmer for 14–16 minutes or until the potatoes are soft.

4 Taste and adjust the seasoning of the soup if necessary, then serve.

Hints and variations You can purée this soup to a smooth consistency in a food processor if you wish.

You can also try adding other vegetables at Step 2, such as celery or even fennel, to give some variations of flavour.

BEST FOR THE FAMILY Hugely rich in magnesium, tomatoes are superb for fortifying bone and cartilage as well as assisting in brain function.

Crispy smoked haddock oat cakes

Fishcakes are a good way to include fish in your family's daily diet – and you can make sure that all those nasty little bones are removed before the children find them. These haddock cakes are great fun to make and served with salad or vegetables they make a perfect family meal.

NOT SUITABLE FOR FREEZING

MAKES 8–10 MEDIUM FISHCAKES

900 g/2 lb potatoes, peeled and cut into small chunks

400 g/14 oz smoked haddock fillets

300 ml/½ pt/1¼ cups milk

60 ml/4 tbsp unrefined sunflower oil

1 large onion, peeled and chopped

10 ml/2 tsp paprika

30 ml/2 tbsp chopped fresh coriander (cilantro)

Juice of ½ lemon

Sea salt and freshly ground black pepper

1 large egg, beaten

100 g/4 oz/1 cup porridge oats

1 Cook the potatoes in lightly salted boiling water for 15–20 minutes or until tender.

2 Meanwhile, put the smoked haddock in large shallow microwave-safe dish and pour over the milk.

3 Cover with clingfilm (plastic wrap) and pierce a few times, then microwave on High (100 per cent power) for 4–5 minutes or until the flesh flakes easily. Alternatively, poach the fish in the milk in a pan, on the hob.

4 Meanwhile, heat 15 ml/1 tbsp of the oil in a frying pan (skillet) and sauté the onion and paprika for about 5 minutes until the onion is soft. Remove from the heat.

5 When the potatoes and fish are ready, drain them both. Mash the potatoes, and remove any skin and bones from the fish.

6 Mix the mashed potatoes, the fish and onions with the coriander and lemon juice and add salt and pepper to taste.

7 Divide the mixture into eight portions. Roll each one into a ball and flatten slightly. Dip into the beaten egg, then coat with the oats.

8 Heat half of the remaining oil in a non–stick frying pan until very hot. Cook four of the fish cakes gently for 2–3 minutes on each side, turning once, until they are golden and crisp.

9 Remove from the pan and drain on kitchen paper (paper towels) while you cook the remaining cakes in the rest of the oil.

Hints and variations You can use frozen haddock fillets if you prefer.

BEST FOR THE FAMILY Oats act as a highly effective tonic to the nervous system and are thought to help calm restless, frustrated children and little ones who may suffer from hyperactivity.

Tuna and tomato cutlets

Fish is such an important food for children to eat. Unfortunately, it's not always popular, except in fish fingers! However, tuna seems to be the exception. These tuna cutlets are very easy to mould, so it's a great idea to let the children make their own shapes – as long as they have washed their hands!

SUITABLE FOR FREEZING

MAKES 4 ADULT PORTIONS

200 g/7 oz/small can of tuna in oil

125 g/4½ oz/good 2 cups fresh wholemeal breadcrumbs

1 large egg, beaten

15 ml/1 tbsp chopped fresh parsley

50 g/2 oz/¼ cup grated full-fat Cheddar cheese

15 ml/1 tbsp tomato purée (paste)

30 ml/2 tbsp unrefined sunflower oil

1 Tip the tuna and oil into a mixing bowl and stir in the breadcrumbs, egg and parsley.

2 Add the grated cheese and tomato purée and bind the mixture together.

3 Mould into small flat cutlet shapes, or fish shapes if you like. If the mixture is too wet to mould, then add more breadcrumbs. If it is a little too dry and crumbly, then add more beaten egg.

4 Heat a little oil in a large non-stick frying pan (skillet). Gently place the cutlets in and cook for 2 minutes on each side.

Serving suggestions Serve these fish cutlets with pasta, vegetables or even mixed salad for a deliciously light lunch or dinner. The children will want tomato ketchup (catsup) with them, of course, but don't let them ladle too much on – it contains masses of sugar.

BEST FOR THE FAMILY I always use wholemeal breadcrumbs in preference to white – they have far more taste and texture as well as containing more nutrients. To make them, put slices of wholemeal bread in a food processor and blend. They can be stored in the freezer for future use.

Salmon and tomato bake

It is wise to encourage your family to taste as many different ways of eating fish as possible in their early years. This will help them to understand and appreciate the many levels of taste and texture that can be achieved from the different methods of cooking that are used.

NOT SUITABLE FOR FREEZING

MAKES 4–6 ADULT PORTIONS

250 g/9 oz penne pasta

300 g/11 oz broccoli, cut into medium-large florets

25 g/1 oz/2 tbsp butter

25 g/1 oz/¼ cup plain (all-purpose) flour

600 ml/1 pt/2½ cups milk

8 sun-dried tomatoes, thinly sliced

100 g/4 oz/½ cup Mascarpone or full-fat cream cheese

1 small bunch of fresh basil leaves, roughly chopped

Sea salt and freshly ground black pepper

4 salmon fillets, about 100 g/4 oz each, skinned and boned

50 g/2 oz/¼ cup grated full-fat mature Cheddar cheese

1 Preheat the oven to 190°C/375°F/gas 5/fan oven 170°C. Grease a large, shallow ovenproof dish.

2 Bring a large pan of lightly salted water to the boil, add the penne pasta and cook according to the packet instructions.

3 When the pasta is almost ready, add the broccoli to the same water to cook for a couple of minutes until just tender.

4 Drain the pasta and broccoli into a colander and drain well.

5 Melt the butter in another large pan and stir in the flour to make a smooth paste. Slowly add the milk, whisking all of the time over a gentle heat, until you have a smooth, silky sauce. Remove from the heat and stir in the tomatoes, Mascarpone or cream cheese and basil. Add the broccoli and pasta and then season well.

6 Halve the salmon fillets lengthways (you'll be able to see an obvious divide on each fillet.)

7 Place the pieces in a single layer in the base of the dish. Spoon the broccoli mixture on top and then scatter with grated cheese.

8 Bake in the preheated oven for 30 minutes or until the dish starts to bubble round the edges. Don't allow the topping to become too dark or else the fish will overcook and be a little dry.

9 Remove from the oven and leave to cool slightly before serving.

Hints and variations To save time, the dish can be prepared in advance up to the end of Step 6. Store overnight in the fridge and reheat the following day.

BEST FOR THE FAMILY The thing that most puts children off eating fish is the small pin bones. These can easily be removed: simply run the back of knife along the surface of the fish to find them, and then remove with tweezers.

FEEDING THE FAMILY: A SOCIAL EXPERIENCE

Honey and orange prawn stir-fry

A simple stir-fry is one of the tastiest and most nutritious meals to feed your family and is a brilliant choice if you're short of time to prepare a meal. All you need is a good-quality wok or a large non-stick frying pan. The key is to have plenty of room inside the pan to keep all of the ingredients on the move.

NOT SUITABLE FOR FREEZING

MAKES 4 ADULT PORTIONS

200 g/7 oz packet of rice or egg stir-fry noodles

15 ml/1 tbsp clear honey

15 ml/1 tbsp soy sauce

2 cloves of garlic, peeled and crushed

Juice and zest of 1 orange

200 g/7 oz thawed frozen cocktail prawns (shrimp)

30 ml/2 tbsp unrefined sesame oil

100 g/4 oz/2 cups beansprouts

1 bunch of spring onions (scallions), finely chopped

1 red (bell) pepper, sliced

1 yellow pepper, sliced

1 green pepper, sliced

225 g/8 oz bag of baby spinach leaves

1 Bring a pan of water to the boil and cook the noodles according to the instructions on the packet. (Boiling the water in a kettle first makes this super-quick!)

2 Whisk together the honey, soy sauce, garlic and orange juice and zest. Add the prawns and stir to coat completely, then leave to marinate.

3 Heat half of the sesame oil in a wok or large frying pan (skillet) and then add all of the vegetables, except the spinach.

4 Stir-fry quickly for a couple of minutes, then add the prawns and their marinade, stirring well. When the prawns are hot through, remove the pan from the heat.

5 Mix the spinach leaves with the noodles and pour any excess juice from the stir-fry into them.

6 Tip into warm bowls and top with the prawn stir-fry.

Serving suggestions This tastes just as good cold – try it as a tasty lunchbox salad for a change from sandwiches.

Hints and variations You can replace the prawns with small strips of chicken or pork, or for a vegetarian stir-fry you could try tofu or crushed cashew nuts.

BEST FOR THE FAMILY Do support your local suppliers of farm-fresh or organic meats and fish. You will certainly taste the difference in food from a happy creature that has had fresh air and sunshine during its life and has not been treated with a range of chemicals and antibiotics.

Hash browns with melted Emmental cheese

*Sunday is the ideal day to enjoy a family meal around the table and if you've
managed to have a lie-in and it's getting close to lunch, then Sunday brunch is a
great idea. Of course, it works just as well if the baby has had you up since 5 am!
These hash browns with melted cheese taste great and will be a real favourite.*

SUITABLE FOR FREEZING

MAKES 4 ADULT PORTIONS

4 medium starchy potatoes

25 g/1 oz/2 tbsp butter, melted

10 ml/2 tsp dried parsley

50 g/2 oz/¹⁄₂ cup plain (all-purpose) flour

**Sea salt and freshly ground
black pepper**

**125 g/4¹⁄₂ oz/good 1 cup grated full-fat
Emmental (Swiss) cheese**

15 ml/1 tbsp unrefined sunflower oil

1 Part-cook the potatoes whole in a pan of boiling water for
6–8 minutes. Drain in a colander and leave to cool.

2 When cold enough to handle, peel the potatoes and coarsely grate
them into a bowl. Mix the melted butter in a small dish with the
parsley. Add this to the potatoes and stir well.

3 Add the flour, season with salt and pepper and mix well. Divide the
potato mixture into four equal-sized pieces and then flatten each
one.

4 Place some grated cheese in the middle of each portion, then fold
over and press down the sides to seal.

5 Heat the oil in a non-stick frying pan (skillet) and cook the hash
browns for about 3 minutes on each side until golden all over.

6 Serve while still warm, before the cheese can cool and harden.

Hints and variations You can precook the hash browns and then
reheat them in a moderate oven for about 12–15 minutes. For a
change, put chopped ham or other cheeses into the middle.

BEST FOR THE FAMILY Cheese can help combat tooth decay caused by
sugary foods. It seems to work by preventing the formation of acids in the
mouth, which attack the enamel on teeth.

FEEDING THE FAMILY: A SOCIAL EXPERIENCE

Sweet and sour chicken casserole

Children often enjoy the contrasting tastes of sweet and sour. Achieving a really good balance of the two flavours is a bit of an art – and small children will be put off if there's too much of the latter. But once you've learnt the basic method you can add anything you like and make your own unique dishes.

SUITABLE FOR FREEZING

MAKES 6 ADULT PORTIONS

1 bunch of spring onions (scallions), coarsely chopped

2 garlic cloves, peeled

1 red (bell) pepper, seeded

450 g/1 lb boneless chicken, diced

30 ml/2 tbsp light soy sauce

10 ml/2 tsp dried ginger

15 ml/1 tbsp unrefined sunflower oil

15 ml/1 tbsp white wine vinegar

15 ml/1 tbsp unrefined soft brown sugar

225 g/8 oz/small can of diced pineapple in natural juice

10 ml/2 tsp cornflour (cornstarch)

150 ml/¼ pt/⅔ cup orange juice

1 Place the spring onions, garlic and pepper in a food processor and blend until completely chopped up.

2 Sprinkle the chicken with the soy sauce and ginger and stir well.

3 Heat the oil in a large frying pan (skillet), then add the chicken and sauté until golden.

4 Add the chopped vegetables and continue to cook.

5 Put the vinegar, sugar and the pineapple and its juice into a separate pan. Mix the cornflour with the orange juice until smooth. Add this to the pan and whisk well over a moderate heat until the sauce thickens.

6 Pour the sweet and sour sauce into the pan with the chicken and mix well.

7 Serve hot.

Serving suggestions Stir-fries can be served on a bed of rice, or egg or rice noodles.

Hints and variations You can use this sauce to make any sweet and sour casserole that you like. It works well with chunks of pork and firm fish. For a vegetarian version, use tofu or meat substitute and cook as per the method above.

BEST FOR THE FAMILY A recent study of the most popular fast foods revealed that Chinese take-away came up as the second unhealthiest. This was largely due to the vast amounts of monosodium glutamate, hydrogenated fat and refined sugar used in its preparation. It is fair to say that not all Chinese fast-food establishments use these products but it still makes sense not to overdo the take-aways!

Mushroom stroganoff

Toddlers and children either love or hate mushrooms! It's usually the texture ('slimy') or colour ('dirty') that puts them off. However, I have had great success with this dish with many youngsters. It is incredibly quick, provided that you have the simple ingredients to hand.

MAKES 4–6 PORTIONS

15 ml/1 tbsp unrefined sunflower oil

½ onion, peeled and finely chopped

400 g/14 oz button mushrooms, sliced

25 g/1 oz/2 tbsp butter

2 garlic cloves, peeled and crushed

200 ml/7 fl oz/scant 1 cup full-fat plain Greek yoghurt

15 ml/1 tbsp finely chopped fresh parsley

100 ml/3½ fl oz/scant ½ cup double (heavy) cream

5 ml/1 tsp Dijon mustard

Sea salt and freshly ground black pepper

1 Heat the oil in a large frying pan (skillet). Add the chopped onion and sauté for 1 minute.

2 Add the sliced mushrooms and butter, then the garlic. Continue to cook for a further minute before adding the yoghurt, parsley, cream and mustard.

3 Season to taste before serving.

Serving suggestions This dish is delicious served as a filling for the Perfect Baked Potatoes on page 115. Alternatively, try spreading it on buttered toast for an inexpensive family supper.

BEST FOR THE FAMILY Many types of mushrooms are well documented to have healing qualities. Even the common button mushroom used in this recipe has been found to help reduce the fat level in blood. Research into mushrooms is continually making valuable new discoveries.

Parsnips and potatoes with rosemary cream

Parsnips and potatoes cooked together are a perfect marriage, with the parsnips adding a gentle sweetness to the combination. In this recipe I've added garlic, cream and some rosemary to enhance the flavour of both these wonderful vegetables, and the cheese gives it a lovely golden appearance.

SUITABLE FOR FREEZING

MAKES 4–6 ADULT PORTIONS

4 medium potatoes, peeled and sliced

4 medium parsnips, sliced as thinly as possible

175 ml/6 fl oz/³⁄₄ cup double (heavy) cream

175 ml/6 fl oz/³⁄₄ cup milk

3 garlic cloves, peeled and crushed

10 ml/2 tsp dried rosemary

A pinch of grated nutmeg

A pinch of sea salt

A pinch of cayenne

50 g/2 oz/¹⁄₄ cup grated full-fat Red Leicester cheese

1 Preheat the oven to 180°C/350°F/gas 4/fan oven 160°C. Grease a shallow baking dish.

2 Put a layer of sliced potatoes and parsnips in the base of the dish.

3 Mix together the cream, milk, garlic, rosemary, nutmeg, salt and cayenne. Pour a little of this mixture over the vegetables in the dish. Continue to add layers of vegetables, pouring a little of the milk mixture over each, until you reach the top of the dish. Cover with the grated cheese.

4 Set the dish on a baking (cookie) sheet and put into the oven.

5 Bake for 40–45 minutes until tender (test with a knife).

6 Serve hot.

Hints and variations You can use other herbs, such as sage or thyme, or even try adding a little chilli to spice this dish up.

If your child doesn't eat enough vegetables, try mixing half coarsely grated Red Leicester cheese with half finely grated carrots and serve as a red cheese sandwich – he'll never know!

BEST FOR THE FAMILY Research indicates that parsnips may help to clear the liver and gall bladder of obstructions. They have also been shown to help lubricate the intestines and reduce wind. This is due to the fact that parsnips are rich in concentrated silicon.

Savoury cheese and spinach pudding

Cheese and spinach are a classic combination and in this dish they are perfectly combined to make a satisfying savoury pudding. Once you are confident with this recipe why not try using different cheeses – blue cheese makes a more tangy version – or a chunkier vegetable, such as broccoli.

SUITABLE FOR FREEZING

MAKES 4–6 ADULT PORTIONS

6 large eggs

425 ml/14½ fl oz/good 1¾ cups milk

10 ml/2 tsp Dijon mustard

A pinch of sea salt

A pinch of cayenne

200 g/7 oz bread, cut into 3 thick slices

200 g/7 oz/scant 1 cup grated full-fat mature Cheddar cheese

225 g/8 oz packet of frozen spinach, thawed

1 Preheat the oven to 190°C/375°F/gas 5/fan oven 170°C.

2 Break the eggs into a food processor and pour in the milk. Add the mustard, salt and cayenne.

3 Tear up the slices of bread, add to the processor and then whizz together until smooth. Tip the mixture into a large bowl and add two-thirds of the cheese.

4 Squeeze the spinach to remove any excess water and then add the leaves to the mixture. Turn into a large baking dish. Top with the remaining cheese.

5 Bake in the oven for 30–35 minutes until risen and golden brown.

6 Serve hot.

Serving suggestions I like to serve this with a freshly mixed salad and some steamed potatoes.

BEST FOR THE FAMILY Spinach contains high levels of the plant form of vitamin A, needed for healthy skin and excellent for improving eyesight in general.

No-nonsense kedgeree

Kedgeree is a great favourite in my family and makes an extremely nutritious, uncomplicated meal. Once you've mastered the basic techniques you can start to add other ingredients to give a little variation. Remember to remove all the pin bones from the fish.

SUITABLE FOR FREEZING

MAKES 4–6 ADULT PORTIONS

125 g/4½ oz/good ½ cup long-grain rice

500 g/18 oz smoked haddock fillet

150 ml/¼ pt/⅔ cup double (heavy) cream

2.5 ml/½ tsp ground turmeric

2 eggs

50 g/2 oz/¼ cup butter

1 medium onion, peeled and sliced

10 ml/2 tsp mild curry powder

Sea salt

A pinch of cayenne

15 ml/1 tbsp chopped fresh coriander (cilantro)

1 Bring a large pan of lightly salted water to the boil and cook the rice for about 15 minutes until tender.

2 Meanwhile, place the haddock in a medium pan with the cream and ground turmeric. Cover and poach very gently for 5 minutes until the flesh separates when tested with the point of a knife. Gently lift out the fish and reserve the cooking liquid.

3 Hard-boil (hard-cook) the eggs, then peel and roughly chop the whites and yolks. Mix together.

4 Once the rice is cooked, drain well in a colander. Heat the same pan and add the butter, sliced onion and curry powder. Sauté for 2–3 minutes until the onion is soft and aromatic.

5 Remove any bones and skin from the cooked fish and break into big pieces.

6 Tip the rice into the pan of onions along with the reserved cream, some salt and a pinch of cayenne and mix well. Finally add the chopped eggs and flaked haddock, mixing very gently so as not to break up the delicate pieces.

7 Spoon into a serving dish, sprinkle with chopped coriander and serve warm.

Serving suggestions Mango chutney makes a good partner for kedgeree. You need nothing more than a fresh mixed salad to make a satisfying evening meal.

Hints and variations Kedgeree makes a great cold salad as a lunch-box idea.

BEST FOR THE FAMILY Haddock, a member of the cod family, is an excellent food for supporting the body in growth and development because of its high levels of vitamin B_{12}.

Naturally balanced egg-fried rice

Egg-fried rice is really excellent comfort food and perfect for hungry toddlers and small children. Because of the many different colours and textures it is a joy to their all their senses. I've designed this recipe to make a large quantity as egg-fried rice keeps so well in the fridge and freezer.

SUITABLE FOR FREEZING

MAKES 4–6 ADULT PORTIONS

225 g/8 oz/1 cup basmati rice, soaked in water overnight

30 ml/2 tbsp unrefined sesame oil

½ medium onion, peeled and finely chopped

1 red (bell) pepper, cut into small dice

1 yellow pepper, cut into small dice

4 spring onions (scallions), chopped

3 eggs, beaten

90 g/3½ oz/scant 1 cup frozen peas, thawed

15 ml/1 tbsp soy sauce

15 ml/1 tbsp chopped fresh coriander (cilantro)

1 Drain the rice in a colander and give it a good wash. This will release any excess starch.

2 Place in a saucepan of lightly salted boiling water and cook for 10–15 minutes until tender.

3 Meanwhile, heat a large wok or non-stick frying pan (skillet) and add 15 ml/1 tbsp of the sesame oil.

4 Stir-fry the chopped onion, peppers and spring onions for a couple of minutes until softened. Remove from the pan and leave to one side.

5 Once the rice is cooked, drain thoroughly in a colander.

6 Reheat the pan and add the remaining sesame oil. Once the oil is hot, add the rice and keep stirring to prevent the rice from sticking. Cook for 3–4 minutes or until you hear the rice 'popping'.

7 Make a well in the centre of the rice and add the beaten egg, stir quickly to form almost into a scrambled consistency and then gradually combine the rice with the egg.

8 Add the sautéed vegetables and the peas, followed by the soy sauce.

9 Sprinkle the chopped coriander over and serve.

Serving suggestions This is delicious on its own, hot or cold. It is also good as an accompaniment to other stir-fries.

Hints and variations For a young baby's portion, the rice will need to be cooked really well and the vegetables quite finely blended in a food processor.

BEST FOR THE FAMILY Peppers change from green to either red or yellow as they ripen on the vine and become sweeter. Pound for pound, yellow peppers contain three times as much vitamin C as oranges.

Easy vegetable biryani

A biryani is usually described as a dry curry, which often contains a large quantity of cooked rice. Like most curries, it is very versatile – you can add anything you have to hand. The great advantage to this dish is that it tastes fabulous served cold the next day and therefore makes a great lunchbox idea!

SUITABLE FOR FREEZING

MAKES 4–6 ADULT PORTIONS

15 ml/1 tbsp unrefined sunflower oil

1 onion, peeled and finely chopped

10 ml/2 tsp mild curry powder

50 g/2 oz/¹⁄₃ cup sultanas (golden raisins)

300 ml/¹⁄₂ pt/1¹⁄₄ cups hot vegetable stock

250 g/9 oz cooked long-grain rice

1 red (bell) pepper, cut into small dice

1 yellow pepper, cut into small dice

30 ml/2 tbsp korma curry paste

200 g/7 oz/1³⁄₄ cups frozen peas, thawed

Juice of ¹⁄₂ lemon

50 g/2 oz/¹⁄₂ cup roasted and salted cashew nuts

1 Heat the oil in a large non-stick frying pan (skillet). Add the chopped onion and curry powder, then stir for a couple of minutes over a gentle heat until softened and aromatic.

2 Meanwhile, place the sultanas in a medium-sized bowl. Pour the hot stock over and leave to soak.

3 Add the cooked rice and chopped peppers to the pan of onions and sauté on a high heat.

4 Mix the korma paste with the peas and add the lemon juice. Add to the pan of rice and onions. Pour in the sultanas and stock.

5 Bring to the boil, stirring all the time, and then turn down the heat and leave to simmer for 5–6 minutes.

6 Sprinkle the crushed cashew nuts on top and serve the biryani hot.

Hints and variations You can add any cooked meats, poultry or fish to this biryani. Stir in with the cooked rice (Step 3).

BEST FOR THE FAMILY I strongly recommend using brown rice. It does take longer to cook than refined white rice so I suggest that you cook a large amount and freeze it in smaller quantities for future use. It is not advisable to re-freeze rice once you have defrosted it.

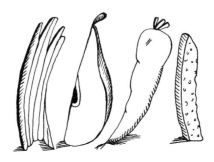

Treacle tart with apricots

This is a variation on that old favourite, warm, home-made treacle tart – a real treat for your young family on a cold winter night. The recipe uses less sugar and instead incorporates apricots for natural sweetness. You could use other dried fruits such as sultanas, peaches or even raisins.

SUITABLE FOR FREEZING

MAKES 6 ADULT PORTIONS

FOR THE PASTRY (PASTE)
115 g/4½ oz/good 1 cup plain (all-purpose) wholemeal flour

115 g/4½ oz/good 1 cup plain white flour

115 g/4½ oz/good ½ cup butter

A pinch of sea salt

About 30 ml/2 tbsp cold water

FOR THE FILLING
60 ml/4 tbsp golden (light corn) syrup

75 g/3 oz/½ cup dried unsulphured apricots, finely chopped

Juice of ½ lemon

50 g/2 oz/1 cup fresh wholemeal breadcrumbs

1 Preheat the oven to 200°C/400°F/gas 6/fan oven 180°C.

2 To make the pastry, using your fingertips, rub the flours, butter and salt together in a bowl to the consistency of breadcrumbs. Bind together with a little cold water.

3 Gently knead the dough and roll out to fit a 23 cm/9 in flan tin (pie pan). Place in the fridge to rest for about 30 minutes.

4 Cover with baking parchment, held down with a handful of dried beans or uncooked rice. Bake blind in the oven for about 15 minutes. Discard the baking parchment and beans or rice.

5 Meanwhile, make the filling. Mix the golden syrup, apricots, lemon juice and breadcrumbs together. Spoon into the cooked pastry base (pie shell).

6 Turn the oven down to 160°C/325°F/gas 3/fan oven 145°C and bake for 25 minutes until golden brown.

7 Serve warm or cold.

Serving suggestions Treacle tart is wonderful with thick custard or crème fraîche. For a lighter touch, try it with some fresh berries.

Hints and variations I like to use half black treacle (molasses) to half golden syrup for an interesting colour and texture.

BEST FOR THE FAMILY Refined sugars pass quickly into our bloodstream and, used in large amounts, can weaken the whole body system. Whenever possible, try to use alternatives such as maple syrup, molasses or fruit juices.

Perfect baked potatoes

One of the best-kept secrets of successful baked potatoes is to cook them on a bed of coarse sea salt. There is no need to prick or brush the potatoes with oil or wrap them in foil – this simple method works perfectly and will help make your jacket potatoes a real family favourite.

NOT SUITABLE FOR FREEZING

MAKES 4 ADULT PORTIONS

4 medium baking potatoes

500 g/18 oz/1¼ cups coarse sea salt

50 g/2 oz/¼ cup butter

Sea salt and freshly ground black pepper

1 Preheat the oven to 200°C/400°F/gas 6/fan oven 180°C.

2 Scrub and wash the potatoes, then pat dry with a kitchen paper (paper towels).

3 Lay the salt crystals in a shallow baking tin (pan) and place the potatoes on top.

4 Bake in the oven for about 1½ hours.

5 Once the potatoes are cooked, brush off any salt. Cut a slice off the top of each potato horizontally. Scoop out the inside with a spoon and place in a bowl with the butter. Season with a little salt and pepper and mash well.

6 Pile the filling back inside the crisp potato shells and then cover with the 'lids'.

7 Serve hot.

Serving suggestions Try filling these potatoes with my Avocado Cream (see page 34) – it makes a delicious alternative to soured (dairy sour) cream.

Hints and variations Sweet potatoes can be baked in their jackets in the same way. The flesh, scooped out and mashed with a little breast or formula milk, can be served to babies of 4–6 months.

To reheat, place in the oven for 10–12 minutes, or pop into the microwave on High (100 per cent power) for 1 minute per potato.

BEST FOR THE FAMILY Potato skins have a delicious, nutty flavour and are full of wonderful nutrients. Encouraging your children to enjoy the skin gives them a great source of fibre and nutrients.

Lighter sticky toffee pudding

This is a perfect treat for all the family and best served in the cold autumn and winter months. Sticky sponge puddings are not exactly everyone's idea of healthy food, but this recipe is much lighter than the traditional version. It can be sliced and served as a cake the next day for lunchbox snacks.

SUITABLE FOR FREEZING

MAKES 6–8 ADULT PORTIONS

FOR THE PUDDING
150 g/5 oz/good ¾ cup stoned (pitted) dates, chopped

120 ml/4 fl oz/½ cup boiling water

100 g/4 oz/½ cup non-hydrogenated margarine

150 g/5 oz/scant ⅔ cup unrefined soft dark brown sugar

2.5 ml/½ tsp natural vanilla essence (extract)

2 large eggs

175 g/6 oz/1½ cups self-raising (self-rising) flour

FOR THE SAUCE
90 g/3½ oz/scant ½ cup butter

150 g/5 oz/scant ⅔ cup unrefined soft dark brown sugar

120 ml/4 fl oz/½ cup double (heavy) cream

1 Preheat the oven to 180°C/350°F/gas 4/fan oven 160°C. Grease and flour a 900 g/2 lb loaf tin (pan).

2 Place the dates in a bowl and pour over the water. Meanwhile, cream the margarine, sugar and vanilla together.

3 Whisk the eggs and gradually beat into the creamed mix.

4 Add the flour, dates and any remaining soaking liquid. Mix gently and then spoon into the loaf tin (it should be about three-quarters full). Gently tap the tin to settle the contents.

5 Bake in the oven for 20–25 minutes until firm to the touch. Remove from the oven and allow to cool for a few minutes before turning out on to a wire rack.

6 To prepare the sauce, melt the butter in a small pan over a gentle heat. Add the sugar and stir until dissolved. Pour in the cream, bring to the boil and cook for 2 minutes until thickened.

7 Slice the toffee pudding and serve with a little toffee sauce poured over the top.

Serving suggestions For extra indulgence, serve with a little vanilla ice cream.

Hints and variations Try experimenting by adding other spices to the mixture (at Step 4). Ground ginger and cinnamon both work very well.

BEST FOR THE FAMILY Hydrogenated fat contains substances called trans fats, which do not exist in nature. In fact, they are so hard you could hold them in your hand all day and they would not melt. Our bodies find it very difficult to process these, so I prefer to use non-hydrogenated fat, as here. There are fats and oils that work with the body in a healing nature, and work to lower blood pressure and protect the body and heart. Ask at your local health food shop for more information.

FEEDING THE FAMILY: A SOCIAL EXPERIENCE

time for sanctuary:

grown-up treats

When you have a baby or a young child in the house, your lifestyle can tend to revolve around them. Your own routine is often governed by their feeds and sleeps – and by the times when you know they'll be feeling grumpy and need lots of attention. The impact of pregnancy and childbirth is obviously huge on the mother, and both parents are on a very steep learning curve, as they try to come to terms with the demands of parenthood, the needs of the newest member of the family and the impact of all these changes within their partnership. If you are bringing up a family on your own, then the pressure can be even greater.

So it's all too easy to forget that you, the grown-ups in the house, need to ensure that your own diet is nutritious and balanced, too, so you have plenty of energy and vitality to cope with your new lifestyle.

Plus it does no harm at all to indulge in a little pampering! So this chapter is dedicated to you, the parents, in honour of all the hard work you have already accomplished and in anticipation of the years of growth ahead.

These recipes have been put together to help you feed body and soul. With a touch of luxury to make you feel a bit special, they are still quick and easy to prepare. Try to make sure you regularly make some space for yourselves, even if it's only once a month. Take the time to enjoy each other's company and re-establish your relationship or, if you are on your own, invite a friend round to share your meal and remind yourself of the pleasures of adult company and conversation at the end of a baby-filled day!

Relax and enjoy.

Chapattis with mango and lime dip

Chapattis are small unleavened Indian bread pancakes. They are incredibly easy to prepare and are delicious as a side dish, on their own or served with dip, as here, to make a delicious late-night snack. There's something very relaxing about eating with your fingers, I think.

SUITABLE FOR FREEZING

MAKES 20–25 CHAPATTIS

100 g/4 oz/1 cup strong plain (bread) flour

100 g/4 oz/1 cup wholemeal (wholewheat) bread flour

10 ml/2 tsp poppy seeds

A pinch of curry powder

A pinch of sea salt

10 ml/2 tsp unrefined sunflower oil

250 ml/8 fl oz/1 cup lukewarm water

A little plain (all-purpose) flour, for dusting

FOR THE DIP

100 ml/3½ fl oz/scant ½ cup full-fat thick plain live yoghurt

Juice of 1 lime

10 ml/2 tsp mango chutney

15 ml/1 tbsp chopped fresh coriander (cilantro)

1 Put the flours, poppy seeds, curry powder and salt in a large mixing bowl and stir together. Add the oil.

2 Gradually stir in the water and mix until the ingredients form a soft dough. If the mixture feels too dry, then add a little more water.

3 Cover the bowl with a damp cloth and leave to stand for 30 minutes.

4 Moisten your hands with a little oil, then shape the dough into 20–25 small balls. Dip the balls in plain flour, then roll out thinly on a floured surface.

5 To cook the chapattis, heat a large non-stick frying pan (skillet), add one or two chapattis to the pan and cook for about 1 minute on each side until dry. Remove from the pan and keep them warm while you cook the remaining chapattis.

6 To make the dip, blend together the yoghurt, lime juice and mango chutney until smooth. Stir in the chopped coriander and spoon into a small pot.

7 Serve the chapattis warm with the dip.

Serving suggestions As an alternative, you can serve the chapattis with my Two-cheese Fondue with Cider (see page 120).

Hints and variations You can add pretty much any type of seed or spice to the basic recipe. You might like to try a few coriander, mustard or sesame seeds, or even a little ground cumin or turmeric.

BEST FOR YOU Make sure you always buy live yoghurt as it contains the beneficial bacteria that keep your digestive system running efficiently. You can buy special products containing these 'friendly bacteria' but live yoghurt has just the same effect.

Two-cheese fondue with cider

I think fondue is a fun dish – there's something very sociable about dipping into a communal pot. It is also easy to prepare. You do need to keep the fondue warm – a fondue kit is a best if you have one, but you can improvise with a plate-warmer or just reheat it in the microwave if necessary.

NOT SUITABLE FOR FREEZING

MAKES 2 ADULT PORTIONS

1 garlic clove, peeled and halved

200 ml/7 fl oz/scant 1 cup dry cider

150 g/5 oz/good ½ cup grated full-fat Emmental (Swiss) cheese

150 g/5 oz/good ½ cup grated full-fat Gruyère (Swiss) cheese

10 ml/2 tsp cornflour (cornstarch)

A little cold water

1 Rub the garlic clove around the inside of a small saucepan, then pour in the cider. Bring to the boil, then simmer gently for 2–3 minutes.

2 Gradually add the cheeses, stirring all the time until they are melted and smooth.

3 Mix the cornflour with a little water until you have a smooth paste, then add it to the melted cheese, stirring continuously. Continue to stir over a gently heat for 3–4 minutes until the mixture thickens.

4 Remove from the heat and pour into a small flameproof dish.

5 Serve with a selection of condiments to dip into the warm, melting fondue (see below).

Serving suggestions You can serve anything you like to dip into the fondue: choose from chunks of French bread; sticks of vegetables such as raw carrot, cucumber, courgette (zucchini), (bell) peppers, etc.; thick slices of fruit, such as apple and pear; and even pickled nuts and vegetables.

BEST FOR YOU Cheese is good for you and it's packed with energy. Some are relatively high in fat, but they make a perfectly healthy part of a good balanced diet and while your children are small you may find you need the extra energy boost that it provides more than they do!

let them join in when you are baking -
they love it

children will be proud to serve their own cooking at mealtimes

Mussels with chilli, coconut and lemon

This is a lovely Thai-style recipe that is so quick and easy to cook, it makes a great late-night dish even after a busy day. Mussels are good value for money as well as being very nutritious. Buy them from a reputable source and look for ones with tightly closed shells and a refreshing sea smell.

SUITABLE FOR FREEZING WHEN COOKED

MAKES 2 LARGE ADULT PORTIONS

750 g/1¾ lb fresh mussels, scrubbed and bearded

15 ml/1 tbsp unrefined sesame oil

1 bunch of spring onions (scallions), finely chopped

1 garlic clove, peeled and crushed

1 red chilli, seeded and finely chopped or shredded

200 ml/7 fl oz/scant 1 cup coconut milk

Juice of 1 lemon

15 ml/1 tbsp chopped fresh coriander (cilantro)

1 Wash the mussels well and discard any that are not tightly closed or do not close when tapped sharply.

2 Heat the largest flameproof casserole dish (Dutch oven) you have and add the sesame oil.

3 Once the oil is hot, add the mussels followed by the spring onions, garlic and chopped chilli. Stir well, then cover and steam over a fairly high heat for 2–3 minutes.

4 Add the coconut milk and lemon juice, cover again and steam for a further 2–3 minutes until all the mussels have opened. Discard any that remain closed.

5 Transfer to a warm serving dish and pour over the cooking liquid. Sprinkle with chopped coriander, then serve.

Serving suggestions For a simple, delicious meal, this needs no more than some warm crusty bread to mop up the juices.

Hints and variations There are three important points to cooking mussels: they must be very fresh; use the largest pan you have; and cook them very quickly. That done, you can add all sorts of other flavour combinations: garlic and white wine; freshly grated ginger root; soy sauce; chopped fresh parsley; or even a splash of sherry.

BEST FOR YOU Mussels are reputed to strengthen the liver and kidneys and nourish the blood.

Parmesan and pea risotto with mint

Children can be a drain on your finances as well as your energies, and you may well find that as your children grow into hungry toddlers there is not a great deal of the household food budget to spend on yourselves. Here's the remedy: a dish that is delicious and inexpensive – a perfect meal to enjoy on a quiet night in.

SUITABLE FOR FREEZING

MAKES 2 ADULT PORTIONS

15 ml/1 tbsp olive oil

1 onion, peeled and finely chopped

2 garlic cloves, peeled and crushed

150 g/5 oz/²/₃ cup arborio or other risotto rice

1 vegetable stock cube

500 ml/17 fl oz/2¼ cups hot water

200 g/7 oz/1¾ cups frozen peas

Juice of ½ lemon

Sea salt and freshly ground black pepper

10 ml/2 tsp chopped fresh mint

25 g/1 oz/2 tbsp freshly grated Parmesan cheese

1 Heat the oil in a large frying pan (skillet), then add the onion and sauté for a couple of minutes until soft.

2 Stir in the garlic and the rice and continue to sauté for a couple of minutes until the grains of rice are shiny and coated in the oil.

3 Dissolve the stock cube in the hot water, then pour one-third of the stock into the pan and stir well. Cook, stirring continuously, until the liquid has been absorbed by the rice.

4 Add a little more stock and cook, still stirring, until it has been absorbed. Continue in this way until all the liquid has been absorbed. This will take about 10 minutes.

5 Stir in the peas and continue to cook for another 6–8 minutes until the rice is creamy and just tender, with a little 'bite'.

6 Stir in the lemon juice and season to taste with salt and pepper. Stir in the mint.

7 Serve on warm plates with Parmesan cheese sprinkled generously over the top.

Serving suggestions You can use the principles of making this risotto to make as many different flavour combinations as you like. The only accompaniment you need is a fresh green salad.

Hints and variations I always keep a block of fresh Parmesan in the fridge. Grated straight into a dish, it tastes much better than the commercially grated tub variety. It lasts for ages – and freezes well – so you won't waste it.

BEST FOR YOU Garlic doesn't just add flavour, it has lots of healthy properties. It is though to have the ability to inhibit some viruses including the common cold, and to promote good circulation.

Smoked haddock and bacon omelette

This dish offers a lovely combination of simple, familiar flavours – the haddock and bacon work tremendously well together. Because it's a healthy option, you can enjoy it without any of the guilt that sometimes comes with comfort dishes! You'll find the portions are fairly generous.

NOT SUITABLE FOR FREEZING

MAKES 2 ADULT PORTIONS

2 potatoes, peeled and cut into dice

15 ml/1 tbsp olive oil

½ onion, peeled and finely chopped

4 rashers (slices) of smoked back bacon, chopped

1 garlic clove, peeled and crushed

100 g/4 oz smoked haddock, skinned and cut into small pieces

4 large eggs

50 ml/2 fl oz/3 tbsp milk

25 g/1 oz/2 tbsp butter

A pinch of cayenne

Sea salt and freshly ground black pepper

A pinch of grated nutmeg

15 ml/1 tbsp chopped fresh parsley

1 Preheat the oven to 200°C/400°F/gas 6/fan oven 180°C.

2 Bring a medium pan of lightly salted water to the boil and cook the diced potatoes for 7–8 minutes, then drain.

3 Heat the olive oil in a non-stick ovenproof frying pan (skillet). Add the chopped onion and bacon and gently sauté for 2–3 minutes. Add the crushed garlic, the haddock and the cooked potatoes. Continue to cook gently for a further minute, stirring to make sure that all the ingredients are well mixed together.

4 Beat the eggs with the milk, butter, cayenne and a little salt, pepper and nutmeg, then pour into the frying pan.

5 Place in the oven for 10–12 minutes until the top is golden and firm to the touch, but still with a little 'give'.

6 Cut into wedges and sprinkle with parsley before serving.

Serving suggestions This makes a simple, satisfying meal served with a crisp green salad and some crusty bread.

Hints and variations You can use any kind of cooked potato for this dish – except mash, of course!

BEST FOR YOU White fish is a very good source of calcium. We all know that calcium is associated with strong bones and teeth but it is also excellent for helping nerves and muscle tissues to function effectively.

Easy bouillabaisse

I have to admit that this is not my creation but I've tasted it many times and it's truly delicious. If you like this recipe, then the compliments go to my friend Andy. If you're not happy with it, then the complaints go to him as well! The quantity allows for second helpings – or, if you can resist, some leftovers for the next day.

SUITABLE FOR FREEZING

MAKES 2 ADULT PORTIONS

15 ml/1 tbsp olive oil

1 large onion, peeled and finely chopped

2 garlic cloves, peeled and crushed

2 x 400 g/14 oz/large cans of chopped tomatoes

500 ml/17 fl oz/2¼ cups vegetable stock

1 bouillon cube

1 red (bell) pepper, chopped

1 green pepper, chopped

1 yellow pepper, chopped

Grated zest of 1 orange

A large pinch of ground saffron

7.5 ml/1½ tsp dried Italian mixed herbs such as oregano, basil and parsley

5 ml/1 tsp unrefined caster (superfine) sugar

Sea salt and freshly ground black pepper

700 g/1½ lb white fish such as cod, coley, monkfish or sea bass, cut into medium-sized chunks

100 g/4 oz cooked peeled prawns, thawed if frozen

2.5 ml/½ tsp cayenne

30 ml/2 tbsp chopped fresh coriander (cilantro)

1 Heat the oil in a large saucepan and sauté the onion for a few minutes until transparent.

2 Add the crushed garlic and cook briefly.

3 Add the diced tomatoes with their juice, the stock and bouillon cube, then add the chopped peppers.

4 Add the orange zest, saffron, Italian herbs and sugar. Simmer for about 20 minutes until the flavours are well blended but the peppers are not too soft. Set aside until you are nearly ready to serve.

5 About 15 minutes before serving, preheat the grill (broiler) to maximum.

6 Bring the broth to a gentle simmer, then check and adjust the seasoning to taste.

7 Lay the fish and prawns in a shallow baking tin (pan) and season with a little salt and the cayenne. Cook under the preheated grill for 8–10 minutes until the fish flakes when tested with a fork.

8 To serve, ladle the broth into warm serving bowls, add the fish and prawns and scatter the coriander over the top.

Serving suggestions All this needs is some warm French bread.

Hints and variations Use paprika instead of cayenne if you prefer a milder flavour.

BEST FOR YOU This is a classic Mediterranean dish. It is no wonder that the Mediterranean diet is one of the healthiest in the world as it is packed full of nutrients. If you follow a Mediterranean style in your cooking, you'll find it is an excellent way to encourage the younger members of your family to follow a healthy balanced diet and to enjoy their five-a-day fruit and vegetable target.

Crêpes with lemon and lime

Don't be put off by the fancy French name – crêpes are just pancakes and they are very easy to make. They are also extremely versatile and freeze beautifully. They make a perfect dessert teamed with fruits and other fillings, or you can use them as a quick sweet or savoury snack for your family.

SUITABLE FOR FREEZING

MAKES 4 ADULT PORTIONS

2 eggs

150 ml/¼ pt/⅔ cup milk

150 ml/¼ pt/⅔ cup water

A pinch of sea salt

125 g/4½ oz/good 1 cup plain (all-purpose) flour

Unrefined sunflower oil, for cooking

Juice of 1 lime

Juice of ½ lemon

30 ml/2 tbsp icing (confectioners') sugar

1 Beat the eggs with the milk and water and add a tiny pinch of salt to bring out the flavour.

2 Sift the flour into a bowl and add the liquid gradually, beating all the time. This is easier with an electric mixer but can be done by hand with a balloon whisk.

3 Rub a large non-stick frying pan with a piece of kitchen paper (paper towel) that has been dipped in the oil. (This reduces the amount of fat used.)

4 Heat the pan until very hot, then quickly pour in enough batter to cover the base of the pan in a thin layer when swirled around.

5 Cook until the sides of the pancake start to lift from the pan and turn crisp, then turn the pancake over. This can be done with a spatula but it's much more fun to toss it by flicking up in the air and hoping that you catch it again in the pan the other way up!

6 Squeeze over the lime and lemon juices, then fold the pancake into quarters. Keep warm while you cook the remainder of the batter in the same way.

7 Transfer the crêpes to warm plates and cover generously with sifted icing sugar.

Serving suggestions These are perfect served with vanilla ice cream.

Hints and variations If you decide to serve these at a family meal, the lemon and lime juice will be too sharp for toddlers. Use some puréed fruit instead and perhaps some thick custard (buy ready-made or see page 97).

BEST FOR YOU Sugar tends to sap vitamin C from the body. As lemons and limes are very high in vitamin C, they will help balance the sugar content both in terms of nutrition and taste.

Simple tiramisu

Over the years I have had so many recipes for tiramisu handed down to me. Some are too rich; some are too heavy and most are overly complicated. This recipe is none of these: it is very light and simple, as a classic dessert should be. It's not really worth making a smaller quantity.

NOT SUITABLE FOR FREEZING

MAKES 4 ADULT PORTIONS

150 ml/¼ pt/⅔ cup strong black coffee, preferably espresso

100 ml/3½ fl oz/scant ½ cup amaretto liqueur

8–10 sponge (lady) fingers or amaretti biscuits (cookies)

250 g/9 oz/good 1 cup Mascarpone cheese

250 ml/8 fl oz/1 cup thick custard, ready-made or see page 97

50 g/2 oz/½ cup coarsely grated plain (semi-sweet) chocolate

50 g/2 oz/½ cup toasted flaked (slivered) almonds

1 Mix together the coffee and amaretto liqueur and pour into a shallow dish. Dip the biscuits in the liquid.

2 Take half of the soaked biscuits and put in the bases of four wine glasses, pushing them to the bottom of the glasses.

3 Mix together the Mascarpone and custard. Use half of this mixture to divide among the glasses, pouring it carefully into each one.

4 Sit the remaining biscuits on the Mascarpone mix and sprinkle with half of the grated chocolate. Top with the remaining Mascarpone mix.

5 Chill for at least 3 hours or preferably overnight.

6 When ready to serve, sprinkle with the toasted almonds and the remaining grated chocolate.

Hints and variations For a change, try using whisky or brandy instead of the Amaretto liqueur.

To toast flaked almonds, toss in a hot frying pan (skillet) until they turn golden. Do not leave them unattended – they burn very quickly.

BEST FOR YOU If drunk in excess, coffee may be drain the body's resources. However, small quantities can be very beneficial in helping you keep alert and your memory functions accurate.

Mango and passion fruit cocktail

This delicious cocktail is a perfect drink to serve at any time of day. It's refreshing and classy – and yet there's no alcohol in it, which makes it ideal if you're going to have to get up in the night! Mango and passion fruit are such perfect partners that you don't need to add any other fruit.

NOT SUITABLE FOR FREEZING

MAKES 4 GLASSES

1 large ripe mango

2 passion fruit

400 ml/14 fl oz/1¾ cups soya milk

100 ml/3½ fl oz/scant ½ cup coconut milk

Juice of ½ lime

1 Peel the mango and cut the flesh off the stone (pit) in large dice. Place in a blender. Cut the passion fruit in half and scoop the flesh and seeds into the blender.

2 Add the two milks and the lime juice.

3 Blend until smooth, then pour into glasses and serve.

Serving suggestion Add a handful of ice to the blender to help chill the cocktail.

Hints and variations Papaya and passion fruit make another delicious combination.

BEST FOR YOU Both mango and passion fruit are rich in antioxidants, minerals and vitamins. They are known as 'sunshine' fruits because of their colour and where they grow. You can close your eyes while you sip this drink and pretend you are lying on a sunny beach somewhere!

White and dark chocolate fondue

If you enjoyed my cheese fondue, then you will probably like this chocolate one. White chocolate is delicious but often too sweet, dark chocolate is rich and slightly bitter. Here, the two chocolates are rippled together to make a deliciously rich and seductive chocolate feast!

NOT SUITABLE FOR FREEZING

MAKES 2 ADULT PORTIONS

50 g/2 oz white chocolate

50 g/2 oz good-quality plain (semi-sweet) chocolate

300 ml/½ pt/1¼ cups double (heavy) cream

40 g/1½ oz/3 tbsp unsalted (sweet) butter

A few drops of natural vanilla essence (extract)

2.5 ml/½ tsp ground cinnamon

1 Break the two chocolates into small pieces and place in separate bowls.

2 Put half of the cream and half of the butter into each bowl.

3 Add the vanilla to the white chocolate and heat in the microwave on High (100 per cent power) for about 1½–2 minutes, stirring once or twice, until melted.

4 Add the ground cinnamon to the plain chocolate and heat in the microwave in the same way.

5 Stir the separate bowls of chocolate well with a wooden spoon until thick and velvety.

6 Pour the two chocolates into a small serving dish. You can do this either by pouring them at the same time so that you have a dark and white side or by rippling them together to give a marbled effect.

Serving suggestions Serve this with a selection of sweet things to dip in – marshmallows, macaroons, dried figs, almonds, giant sultanas (golden raisins), etc.

Hints and variations Perk this dessert up by adding a little orange or coffee liqueur or even add a touch of whisky. Always buy the best-quality plain chocolate you can find. Look for labels that say '70 per cent cocoa solids'.

BEST FOR YOU Chocolate is rich in B vitamins, which may be why it seems so good at relieving stress and anxiety. It is, however, important to remember that it is the cocoa bean that contains the beneficial ingredients not the high amounts of sugar and vegetable fat in some chocolate. Too much sugar can make you short-tempered, while vegetable fats can often make you feel lethargic because your liver has to work very hard to break them down – neither of which is good news for new parents.

Kiwi and banana energy booster

This is one of the simplest smoothies and probably one the most effective I have come across. It does not take more then 5 minutes to prepare and really gives you a dose of 'get up and go' in the morning – a real boon if you've been up half the night with a fractious infant.

NOT SUITABLE FOR FREEZING

MAKES 2 GLASSES

2 ripe kiwi fruit

1 large banana

300 ml/¹/₂ pt/1¹/₄ cups pure apple juice

Juice of ¹/₂ lemon

1 Peel the kiwi fruit and banana.

2 Place in a blender and add the apple and lemon juices.

3 Liquidise until smooth, then serve immediately.

Hints and variations I do not recommend making this drink the night before as it loses much of its punch and potency. If you are in a rush in the mornings, then you can peel the kiwi fruit, wrap it tightly in clingfilm (plastic wrap) and store in the fridge ready for the morning.

BEST FOR YOU Kiwi fruit are full of chlorophyll, a plant chemical that helps clean and tone the blood. Chlorophyll is also believed to have anti-cancer properties.

Strawberry and rhubarb smoothie

There is nothing more rejuvenating than a freshly made fruit smoothie. But quite often people find preparing the fruit for blending a bit of a chore. This delicious drink needs no chopping or slicing of fruit whatsoever, but it is best to chill all the ingredients before you start.

NOT SUITABLE FOR FREEZING

MAKES 2 GLASSES

200 g/7 oz fresh or frozen strawberries

225 g/8 oz/small can of rhubarb

300 ml/½ pt/1¼ cups fresh orange juice

Juice of 1 lime

1 If using fresh strawberries, wash and remove their green stems. Place the fruit in a blender or food processor. Frozen fruit may be used straight from the freezer.

2 Add the rhubarb and its syrup from the can, then pour in the orange juice and lime juice.

3 Liquidise until all the ingredients are smooth and blended together.

4 Serve chilled in suitable drinking glasses.

Hints and variations If you forget – or don't have time – to chill of the ingredients before making the drink, simply add a handful of ice cubes to the ingredients at Step 2.

BEST FOR YOU The fresh ingredients in this drink are good sources of potassium, which is beneficial for regulating blood pressure. The strawberries also contain a plant chemical, or 'phytochemical', called ellagic acid, which is believed to help protect against some cancers.

Fresh watermelon juice with lime

This is a really rejuvenating drink. It is a welcome reminder of the natural sweetness of fruit and a delicious antidote to the sugariness of commercial soft drinks. And like all the fruit drinks in this chapter, it is an excellent way of getting some of your five-a-day portions of fruit and veg.

NOT SUITABLE FOR FREEZING

MAKES ABOUT 1.5 LITRES/2½ PTS/6 CUPS

1 medium watermelon

1 lime

A handful of ice cubes

1 Using a serrated knife, peel the watermelon and then cut the flesh into chunky dice.

2 Place half of the diced watermelon into a food processor with the half the juice of lime and half the ice. Blend until the melon and ice are completely broken down, then tip the contents through a sieve (strainer) into a bowl. Repeat the same process with the remaining ingredients. (If the mixture does not pass through the sieve easily, then simply use the back of a ladle to push the liquid through. Don't worry if little black specks appear in the juice, it is simply flecks of watermelon seed, which are totally safe to consume.)

3 Serve in tall glasses.

Hints and variations If you place this drink in the freezer and stir occasionally it will turn into an ice slush, which is very refreshing on a hot day.

You can add other ingredients to this basic recipe, such as orange or grapefruit – pink grapefruit is particularly delicious.

BEST FOR YOU This is a drunk as a daily tonic in Morocco, where it is believed to be one of the elixirs of life, promoting health and a clean digestive system.

Tangy vegetable juice

A simple combination of blended vegetables and herbs can make a really delicious savoury drink – another way to make sure you get your daily requirement of vitamins. Once you are confident with this recipe, then you'll be able to experiment using other combinations of ingredients.

NOT SUITABLE FOR FREEZING

MAKES 2 GLASSES

2 celery sticks

6 ripe tomatoes

A few sprigs of fresh coriander (cilantro)

10 ml/2 tsp tomato purée (paste)

10 ml/2 tsp Worcestershire sauce

1–2 dashes of chilli sauce

300 ml/¹/₂ pt/1¹/₄ cups apple juice

Juice of ¹/₂ lemon

1 Chop the celery into small pieces, removing the stringy parts as you go.

2 Chop the tomatoes and coriander and then place in a blender with the tomato purée.

3 Add the Worcestershire and chilli sauces and pour in the apple and lemon juices. Liquidise until smooth and serve immediately.

Hints and variations You can add more tomato purée if you wish – this will deepen the colour of the juice. You can also add a little garlic purée before you blend the vegetables to give a little more kick to the finished drink.

BEST FOR YOU If you are a little 'bunged up', then be sure to dose up with chilli. Chilli contains a phytochemical that can help relieve nasal congestion. This drink is also loaded with vitamin C and other beneficial nutrients to help combat the common cold.

Whisky and honey tea

The recipe for this delicious drink was passed on to me by a friend, who got it from her friend Linda. Linda is a hard-working nurse as well as a successful mother, so she knows how important it is to relax. She found this whisky tea a perfect drink to sit down with during those precious moments of peace.

NOT SUITABLE FOR FREEZING

MAKES 2 TEACUPS

**2 Earl Grey teabags
or 10 ml/2 tsp Earl Grey tea leaves**

15 ml/1 tbsp whisky

10 ml/2 tsp clear honey

Milk, to taste (optional)

1 Boil the kettle, place the tea in a pot and pour over the water. Leave to infuse for 4–5 minutes.

2 Add the whisky and honey and stir gently to dissolve the honey.

3 Strain into cups and add milk to taste, if liked.

4 Drink while sitting down for as long as possible!

Hints and variations Instead of Earl Grey tea, you could use ordinary Indian tea or your favourite herbal infusion.

BEST FOR YOU This is, of course, an alcoholic drink so it is not advised if you are still breastfeeding. However, once your child is past this stage it may be a helpful way of recovering from an energetic toddler!

Spiced cranberry toddy

This is a soothing and uplifting drink, which is ideal to drink during the colder months of the year. You can keep it non-alcoholic or add a shot of vodka if you dare. In the hotter months, you could try chilling this drink to make an interesting and unusual cold beverage.

NOT SUITABLE FOR FREEZING

MAKES 2 GLASSES

250 ml/8 fl oz/1 cup cranberry juice

250 ml/8 fl oz/1 cup apple juice

Juice of 1 lemon

1 cinnamon stick

5 whole cloves

1 piece of star anise

10 ml/2 tsp clear honey

1 Put all the ingredients into a medium saucepan and bring to the boil.

2 Reduce the heat and allow the mixture to simmer for 5 minutes, then turn off the heat. Leave to stand for a further 5 minutes to allow the ingredients to infuse.

3 Strain the liquid through a fine sieve (strainer) and serve in large glasses.

Hints and variations If you want to add a shot of vodka or brandy, then do so only when the heat has been turned off or else you will evaporate the alcohol!

BEST FOR YOU Alcohol is a toxic substance and therefore should be treated with care. This is the reason why it is not recommended for women who are pregnant or breastfeeding. However, I think that this drink is just as delicious without alcohol. Serve it in a wine glass and it will be just as relaxing.

Exfoliating papaya mask

As a special treat, I thought I would include a few healthy cosmetic treats for you to enjoy. Papaya is a great facial friend, containing an enzyme that removes dead skin cells. Oatmeal also works as a great exfoliator so the combination here will leave your skin truly beautifully cleansed.

NOT SUITABLE FOR EATING!

MAKES 1 TREATMENT

100 g/4 oz/1 cup oatmeal

1 papaya (pawpaw), peeled, seeded and mashed

30 ml/2 tbsp clear honey

1 Place the oatmeal in a food processor and grind until it is very fine.

2 Add the mashed papaya and the honey and process to combine everything together well.

3 Apply to the face and neck, avoiding the eyes, and leave for 20 minutes. (Lie down and relax while you can!)

4 Rinse off in warm water.

Banana revitalising mask

This recipe combines ingredients you are bound to have at home and is so quick to whip up you can make it whilst waiting for a cup of tea to brew (make sure you're not expecting visitors though!) The chickpea flour acts as a natural exfoliator whilst the banana will naturally help to soothe and soften your skin.

NOT SUITABLE FOR EATING!

MAKES 1 TREATMENT

60 ml/4 tbsp chickpea (garbanzo) flour

1 banana

1 egg

1 Blend the chickpea flour and banana to a paste.

2 Add the beaten egg and blend until well mixed.

3 Spread the mask on your face and neck, avoiding the eyes, and leave on for 15–20 minutes. Take the time to sit down and relax if you can.

4 Rinse off in warm water.

Citrus sherbet bath tonic

With the combination of refreshing citrus and relaxing lavender, a warm bath with this add makes a perfect way to relax and unwind after an energetic day with your little one. Don't forget to take a good book or magazine and a soothing drink with you to complete the rest cure!

NOT SUITABLE FOR EATING!

MAKES 1 TREATMENT

½ **cup grated orange and lemon zest**

15 ml/1 tbsp chopped fresh parsley

4 drops of lavender essential oil

1 Place all the ingredients in a small piece of muslin (cheese cloth) and tie securely with string or ribbon.

2 Tie the little parcel on to your bath taps so that as you fill the bath the hot water runs through the bag.

3 Lock the bathroom door, lie back and enjoy the fragrant bath.

Fragrant facial steam

I really cannot think of many things as relaxing and cleansing as a good facial steam and this traditional method, using your garden as a treasure chest of beauty products, is still the best in my view. The beauty of this 15-minute indulgence is that it is totally adaptable and can be easily tailored to support you and your partner's preferences.

NOT SUITABLE FOR EATING!

MAKES 1 TREATMENT

A bowl of almost boiling water

A SELECTION OF THESE INGREDIENTS:
A few handfuls of fragrant rose petals or a few drops of rose water

A handful of fresh lavender flowers

A handful of crushed lemon balm leaves

A thinly sliced orange and a squeeze of orange juice

A handful of fresh rosemary stalks, gently crushed

1 Pour the almost boiling water into a large bowl.

2 Sprinkle in your chosen herbs and fragrances.

3 Cover your head with a towel, close your eyes and lean over the bowl. Slowly breathe in the steam vapours for 10–15 minutes, until relaxed and energised.

BEST FOR YOU Many flowers and herbs have specific therapeutic properties. Roses are good for the skin, good for the soul and a wonderful tonic for the mind. Lavender has wonderfully calming properties and is especially effective for nervous tension and related headaches and fatigue. Citrus will bring calm as you breath in the zesty vapours, leaving you feeling refreshed and rejuvenated. Rosemary is uplifting and energising, an all-round excellent tonic.

Index